The Twelve Days of Christmas Cookbook

Suzanne Huntley

Galahad Books · New York City

Drawings by Milton Glaser

Copyright © 1965 by Suzanne Huntley
All rights reserved

Library of Congress Catalog Card Number: 74-77014
ISBN 0-88365-251-X

Published by arrangement with Atheneum

Manufactured in the United States

Designed by Milton Glaser

Suzanne Huntley's

interest in food was inherited from her parents, who enjoyed a reputation for tremendous gustatory curiosity. Born in Washington, D.C., Mrs. Huntley grew up in Florida, has lived in Maryland, Virginia and New Mexico, and has finally settled in Port Hueneme, California, where she lives with her husband. Some years ago she studied domestic science at Briarcliff Junior College in New York, and she was a founding editor and publisher of the *Social List of Fort Lauderdale*.

Author's Note

In the course of compiling this book I ran across mention of a Christmas season dessert enjoyed (?) by Eskimos in Alaska It is said to be composed of "Foamy Seal Blubber with Blueberries." Such exotica have been purposely omitted. (There were no hints on preparation anyway.)

The suggestions which follow, representing many lands and customs, are sometimes bunched together with reckless international abandon. Most of them are the pleasant ghosts of Christmases past, when one or another of the menus was tried with good results.

The recipes have been personally tested, but one remains a dismal failure. If anybody knows the trick of making an uncurdled Tom and Jerry, I would appreciate communication.

S.H.

On the first day of Christmas my true love sent to me
A partridge in a pear tree.

On the second day of Christmas my true love sent to me
Two turtle doves.

On the third day of Christmas my true love sent to me
Three French hens.

On the fourth day of Christmas my true love sent to me
Four calling birds.

On the fifth day of Christmas my true love sent to me
Five gold rings.

On the sixth day of Christmas my true love sent to me
Six geese a-laying.

On the seventh day of Christmas my true love sent to me
Seven swans a-swimming.

On the eighth day of Christmas my true love sent to me
Eight maids a-milking.

On the ninth day of Christmas my true love sent to me
Nine ladies dancing.

On the tenth day of Christmas my true love sent to me
Ten lords a-leaping.

On the eleventh day of Christmas my true love sent to me
Eleven pipers piping.

On the twelfth day of Christmas my true love sent to me
Twelve drummers drumming.

Old English Carol

Contents

CHAPTER ONE

Foresight

On the first day of Christmas my true love sent to me
A partridge in a pear tree.

READY...

More varied situations involving food arise at Christmas than at any other season: gifts of cakes and cookies; tree-trimmers and carolers to be cheered on their way; the last day of Advent; late supper after midnight Mass; *the* dinner itself; parties of all descriptions; the impulsive gesture; and the wind-up Feast of the Epiphany or Twelfth Night. In Latin countries this is the most festive of the holidays, Christmas itself being reserved for religious observation. It is on the night of the Three Kings that children receive their toys, symbolic of the gifts brought to the Christ Child.

In the following menus and recipes you won't find maids a-milking, or swans a-swimming, but some of the foods might set a few lords a-leaping and ladies dancing and there *is* a Partridge in a Pear Tree.

In the midst of card-addressing, decorating and shopping, try to juggle a few hours here and there for advance cooking. Fruit cakes and plum puddings, for instance, can be made weeks, or even months, in advance and are better, anyway, when aged. Fish cookies, the ancient symbol of Christ, can be made ahead of time, and Rum or Bourbon Balls ripen gracefully. The "Indispensable" Smithfield Ham can be prepared ahead; so can a curry for Twelfth Night; and a wonderful stew (frozen without vegetables) can be waiting to meet the demands of the impulsive gesture. Many of the canapé spreads can be frozen, and cheese pastry is actually improved by freezing.

Chestnuts are another thing to "do ahead," and they freeze beautifully; purée some of them in the blender for desserts and leave some whole or coarsely chopped to be added to Brussels sprouts or stuffings.

Check your supply of canned things. Remember potatoes and onions, etc., for the frozen stew in case there is no time when it is served to add fresh ones, and condiments for the curry. Have a good quantity of fruit juices, soups and any family favorites.

SET...

If you are going to need a bartender or waiter or extra help in the kitchen for a party, line them up *early*. I once lived in a medium-sized town where the party schedule depended entirely on the calendar of the one available couple who "helped out." And their calendar for Christmas began filling up in October.

If you need to rent or borrow anything, like a punch bowl or large coffee maker, reserve it as soon as you can; and if your plans call for food or liquor that isn't obtainable locally, work on that as quickly as possible. A whole, large fish, for instance, is sometimes hard to find on the spur of the moment in inland areas but can usually be ordered in advance. Take stock of your local resources and use them: a really fine bakery, perhaps, or a good caterer to do one or two of the heavier chores, like the roasting of a huge bird.

Have a serene, happy and joyful Christmas!

GO...

CHAPTER TWO

Gifts for Your True Love

On the second day of Christmas my true love sent to me
Two turtle doves.

No frankincense, no myrrh, but most of the spices of the Orient go into the following concoctions. All of them serve admirably as gifts, and all of them are good to have around the house.

A Fruitcake which is a particular favorite is made with less flour than usual. I like to leave the fruit and nuts in fairly large pieces, to have the cake well chilled before serving, and to cut it with a sharp, *hot* knife. Chopping the fruit and nuts fine produces a more compact cake and is entirely a matter of individual preference.

The following ingredients will make three loaves, 4½ x 8½ x 2½ inches:

- *1½ cups light brown sugar*
- *1½ cups butter*
- *6 eggs, separated*
- *½ cup each: blanched almonds, walnuts, sultanas, candied cherries*
- *1 cup each: currants, seeded raisins, dates, candied pineapple*
- *1½ cups mixed candied peels*
- *1½ cups flour*
- *1 tablespoon each: mace, cinnamon, cloves, allspice, nutmeg*
- *½ cup brandy or rum*
- *1½ teaspoons baking soda dissolved in a little water (omit at high altitudes)*
- *½ cup sugar syrup or Karo*

Cream the sugar and butter. Add egg yolks, beaten until frothy. Dredge fruit and nuts with half the flour and add gradually to the egg mixture. Add rest of flour, sifted with the spices, then the brandy or rum.

7

Fold in the egg whites, beaten until stiff, and add the soda last.

Line the pans with foil or brown paper and butter the paper liberally. Bake in a very slow oven, 250 to 275 degrees, for 3 ½ to 4 hours, with a pan of water in the bottom of the oven. Cool the cakes, still in the pans, on a rack for about half an hour. Take the cakes out of the pans; carefully remove the lining paper and return the cakes to the rack to cool thoroughly. Decorate the tops with nuts and bits of candied fruit. Dip the bottoms of the decorations in sugar syrup or Karo to make them stay put. Wrap the cakes in cloth soaked in brandy or rum. Store, tightly covered, for *at least* three weeks.

An Uncooked Fruitcake that is quite good (one bread-sized loaf or two small ones) is made this way:

30 graham crackers
½ cup dates, pitted, sliced
½ cup dried apricots, coarsely chopped
¼ cup candied cherries
¼ pound butter
½ cup each: sultanas, chopped nuts, confectioners' sugar, orange marmalade
½ teaspoon salt
1 teaspoon cinnamon
dash of powdered cloves
¼ cup dark rum

Crumb the graham crackers in a blender, six at a time. With the last six crackers add the dates and apricots and blend 15 to 20 seconds on low speed. Put all this in a large bowl and add everything else, mixing well. Pack in an oiled mold or loaf pan and chill 48 hours.

Plum Pudding as a flaming dinner finale is unsurpassed for glamour. Steam it in well-buttered molds or cans with tight covers. Baking-powder tins make nice individual puddings. Fill the molds no more than two-thirds full. Place them on a trivet in a large boiler and add water to half the depth of the mold. Cover and boil rapidly until steam begins to escape, then lower the heat for the rest of the time required to cook them thoroughly.

This recipe makes about 2 quarts of pudding or 12 servings:

> *1 cup kidney suet, finely chopped*
> *1 pound each: seeded raisins, chopped currants*
> *¼ cup preserved citron, chopped*
> *½ cup flour*
> *1 teaspoon mace*
> *½ teaspoon each: nutmeg, cinnamon*
> *3 tablespoons sugar*
> *½ teaspoon salt*
> *4 eggs, separated*
> *2 tablespoons cream*
> *½ cup brandy*
> *1 ½ cups fine dry bread crumbs*
> *1 tablespoon grated lemon rind*

In a large bowl dredge the suet, raisins, currants and citron with half the flour. Sift the rest of the flour together with the spices, sugar and salt and add to the fruit. Beat the egg yolks with the cream until thick and foamy, and beat the egg whites stiff. Add the egg-yolk mixture, bread crumbs and lemon rind to the fruit mixture. Fold in the egg whites last. Pour into buttered molds and steam 3 to 5 hours. Smaller molds will need less time than a large thick one. Unmold the puddings and allow them to cool. Wrap them in brandy-soaked cloths and store, tightly covered, for the same length of time as fruitcake.

Mincemeat or Pâté de Noel, as made in this country, contains meat. In England, no meat. So take your choice. If meat is used, it should be very good-quality boneless beef, well trimmed. Creole cooks sometimes use a mixture of beef and tongue or heart, or all three, and in the West venison is sometimes used. Cook the meat until very tender in unseasoned boiling water, then chop or grind. This recipe makes 4 quarts or, if meat is omitted, about 6½ to 7 pints:

1 pound meat, boiled and chopped fine
½ pound kidney suet, chopped fine
3 large tart apples, peeled, cored and cut in small pieces
1½ teaspoons each: cinnamon, nutmeg, salt
1 teaspoon each: mace, cloves, allspice
1 pound dark brown sugar
1 pint cider
1½ pounds seedless raisins
1 pound currants
½ cup preserved citron, chopped
¼ cup each: candied orange peel, candied lemon peel
1 cup whiskey or brandy

Place the first 11 ingredients (from the meat through the cider) in a large saucepan and bring to a boil. Cook slowly for 45 minutes, stirring frequently. Then add the raisins, currants, citron and citrus peels. Simmer for about an hour, stirring often, until very thick. Add the whiskey or brandy and pack in sterilized jars.

Rum or Bourbon Balls are delicious presents and should be made a couple of weeks ahead of Christmas so that they can ripen nicely. Following is the classic recipe, which will make about 6 dozen balls:

1 cup vanilla-wafer crumbs
1 cup pecans, chopped fine
1 cup powdered sugar

> 2 tablespoons Dutch cocoa
> 1 ½ tablespoons white Karo syrup
> ¼ cup or more rum or bourbon

Mix all ingredients together. Form in small balls, using about 1 rounded teaspoonful of the mixture for each ball. Roll in more powdered sugar and store in a tightly covered container. A variation substitutes gingersnaps or crushed chocolate wafers for the vanilla wafers; if chocolate wafers are used, omit the cocoa. For another variation, use almonds or other nuts. Or roll the balls in cocoa or chopped nuts instead of sugar.

Fish Cookies to hang on the tree are gay creations and fun to make as a family project. The fish, ancient symbol of Christ, is a particularly appropriate shape. If you can find fish-shaped cutters, the job is much easier. I generally make three sizes, cut from cardboard patterns, 2 ½, 3 ½ and 4 ½ inches long. Dividing the dough in equal thirds produces 5 large, 8 medium-sized and 15 or 16 small fish. An especially successful dough is made with:

> 1 cup soft butter
> ½ cup sugar
> 1 egg yolk
> 1 tablespoon grated lemon peel
> 1 teaspoon almond extract
> ¼ teaspoon salt
> 2 to 2 ½ cups all-purpose flour
> blanched almonds, dragées and colored sugar

Cream together the butter and sugar. Beat in the egg yolk. Add the lemon peel, almond extract and salt, and then work in the flour. The dough should be quite stiff. Chill the dough for an hour or so, then roll to ¼-inch thickness on a floured board. Cut and place an inch apart on buttered cookie sheets. Now, take a skewer or toothpick and make a hanging hole at the head end of the fish. Use silver dragées for eyes and whole almonds for scales. I usually use 5 almonds on the 4½-inch cookies, 3 on the 3½-inch and 1 on the smallest. Lightly sprinkle colored sugar over them and bake 10 to 15 minutes in a 350-degree oven. The small ones will take less time than the large ones, so don't mix the sizes on the same baking tin. They should not be brown, but just "set."

When the cookies are cool, cut pieces of narrow ribbon about 9 or 10 inches long. Thread a tapestry needle with the two cut ends. Run through the hanging hole, catch the end loop and pull tight. Small bows of ribbon are gay, especially on the largest fish. Have the bows ready and slip through the loop before pulling tight. Knot together the cut ends of ribbon.

If ants are a problem, or the fish are to be packed and mailed, they can be wrapped in small sheets of self-sticking clear plastic before the hanging ribbon is put on. You may need a dab of Scotch tape to fasten the ends of the plastic.

This dough can be used, of course, for cookies of any shape. Being light-colored, it takes decoration beautifully.

Springerles require a lot of space. They must sit around drying somewhere. And the 24 hours specified in the recipe "ain't necessarily so." If the weather is very humid, they may take as long as 2 days; but in a dry climate 8 to 12 hours is usually enough.

Beautifully carved springerle boards and rolling pins may be considered an extravagance if they are used only once a year; but they are a decorative addition to the kitchen. However, if you don't have these luxuries, you can cut the dough in squares or bars and it will taste just as good. This recipe will make about 60 cookies:

4 eggs
2 cups fine granulated sugar
3½ cups (or more) sifted cake flour
1 teaspoon double-acting baking powder
¼ teaspoon salt
*1 to 2 tablespoons crushed anise seed (roll between
    sheets of wax paper) or 6 drops anise oil*

Beat the eggs and sugar together for 20 minutes. Use a rotary beater or electric mixer on low speed. Sift the flour, baking powder and salt together and work into the first mixture. Dough should be very stiff and may need a little more flour added to it. On a floured board, roll the dough ½ inch thick with a plain rolling pin. Then roll with carved springerle pin, or press the carved board into the dough. Flour the pin or board liberally and bear down hard to make clear impressions. Cut cookies apart as indicated by the patterns. Butter cookie sheets and sprinkle them evenly with the anise seeds. If anise oil is used, add it with the flour; but don't use both seeds and oil. The flavor would be overpowering. Place cookies on prepared pans and allow to dry for 24 hours. Bake about 15 minutes at 325 degrees. These, like the fish cookies, should not be allowed to brown.

Ginger Cookies The basic dough can be cut in any shape and decorated gaily. Or "men" can be made by shaping the dough into balls and cylinders of various sizes and pressing them together: a large ball for the body, a smaller one for the head and long, thin rolls for arms and legs. (These are easy for children to manage and seem to have a direct relationship to mud pies.) Give the "men" faces and suit buttons of raisins,

cherries and nuts. After they are baked, add more em-
bellishments with a paste made of confectioners' sugar
dampened with a little water; apply the paste with a
toothpick or small brush. This recipe will make 8 to
10 fat "men" about 5 inches long, or 50 to 60 small,
thin cookies:

> ¼ *cup butter*
> ½ *cup brown sugar*
> ½ *cup dark molasses*
> 3½ *cups flour, sifted*
> ¼ *cup hot water*
> ¼ *teaspoon powdered cloves*
> 1 *teaspoon each: baking soda,*
>   *salt, ground ginger*
> ½ *teaspoon cinnamon*
> *raisins, nuts, cherries, etc., for décor*

Blend the butter and sugar and beat in the molasses.
Sift together all the dry ingredients and add to molasses mixture, in thirds, alternately with the hot water.
Chill the dough 2 or 3 hours or longer. Roll thin on
a floured board or shape into men. Bake 8 to 10 minutes at 350 degrees on a greased and floured cookie
sheet.

Egg Paint is a fine decorating medium for all the
cookies mentioned and can be applied either before
or after baking. It is usually easier for children to
decorate baked cookies than unbaked ones, though the
temptation to eat them is greater too.

Mix an egg yolk with a few drops of water. Put
portions in tiny dishes and add vegetable colors. Use
a separate soft brush for each color.

Mock Marzipan is another good project for children. They have a wonderful time shaping and coloring the tiny fruits and vegetables; and the ingredients are inexpensive, so if they turn into a mud-colored mess, not much is lost.

1 medium-sized potato
salt
vegetable colors or egg paint
2 1-pound boxes confectioners' sugar
½ cup ground almonds
1 teaspoon (or more) almond extract

Peel the potato, boil, drain and mash it. Add a little salt and mix in the sugar until the mixture becomes creamy, like fondant. The amount of sugar needed depends on the size and moisture of the potato. Be sure to have enough sugar on hand and keep adding until the right texture is achieved. Add the ground almonds and almond extract. Shape into small fruits and vegetables. Color with vegetable coloring or egg paint and set on wax paper to dry before storing in tightly covered containers.

Ice-Cream-Cone Trees make charming table decorations, especially for children's parties. The following amount of icing will do 10 to 12 cones:

3 cups confectioners' sugar
1 unbeaten egg white
½ teaspoon lemon juice
water

Mix ingredients until smooth, using only enough water to make mixture of proper spreading consistency. Cover cones with icing ¼ inch thick. Trim the trees with any assortment of small glittery bits your imagination dictates: cinnamon and other small hard candies, silver dragées, popcorn, candied fruits and colored sugars. These must be put on while the icing is still moist, so frost only one or two cones at a time and keep the remaining icing covered while decorating. Toward the end you may have to add a little more water.

These cones can also be used as cornucopias for your tree. Before frosting, tie a string or ribbon around the base of the cone, leaving ends long enough to loop on the tree. Fill the cones with candy or cookies, or even small presents.

Cinnamon Nuts make delicious nibbling material and are nice presents too. First roast 2½ to 3 cups of nuts for about 15 minutes in a 375-degree oven, stirring frequently to prevent burning. Use walnuts or pecans or whole blanched almonds. Then make a syrup of the following ingredients and cook slowly until a drop of syrup forms a soft ball when plunged in cold water (235 degrees on a candy thermometer).

> *1 cup sugar*
> *½ cup water*
> *1 teaspoon (or more) cinnamon*
> *1 teaspoon salt*

Remove from heat and beat until the mixture looks creamy. Add 1½ teaspoons vanilla and then add the cooled nuts, coating them well. Turn onto a buttered platter and separate them as they cool.

Date Roll is easy to do and keeps well in the refrigerator.

3 cups sugar
1 cup evaporated milk
1 cup dates, pitted and chopped
1 cup nuts (walnuts, pecans, cashews, etc.), chopped

Boil the sugar and milk to the soft-ball stage (235 degrees on a candy thermometer). Then stir in the dates and nuts. Allow to cool. Butter a sheet of foil lightly and dust with confectioners' sugar. Form the mixture into a roll about 1½ inches in diameter and wrap in the prepared foil. Chill until firm and slice fairly thin with a hot knife.

Candied Citrus Peel is another thing that takes a lot of space to prepare but is worth the trouble. Press the fruits (orange, lemon, grapefruit, etc.) lightly on a grater to release some of the oil. Don't grate, just press lightly. Then remove the peel in large pieces Cover the peel with cold water in a saucepan, bring to a boil and simmer for 10 minutes. Repeat this, using fresh water, until peel is tender. About three times usually does it. Cut peel into strips with scissors or into fancy shapes with tiny cookie cutters. For each cup of peel, make this syrup:

½ cup granulated sugar
¼ cup water

Add the peel and boil until it is transparent and all the syrup is absorbed. Shake the peel in a heavy paper bag with granulated sugar and spread on racks to dry.

Mock Stollen makes a lovely addition to Christmas breakfasts or any other breakfast. This recipe makes one "normal-sized" loaf:

½ *cup milk*
¼ *cup sugar*
1 teaspoon salt
3 tablespoons butter
¼ *cup warm water*
1 cake compressed yeast
cooking oil
1 egg, beaten
3 cups (or more) sifted flour
½ *cup blanched almonds, chopped*
½ *cup mixed candied fruits, chopped*
1 teaspoon lemon rind, grated
2 tablespoons sugar
pinch of cardamon

Scald the milk and add the ¼ cup of sugar, salt and 2 tablespoons of butter. Cool this to lukewarm. In a bowl dissolve the yeast in warm water; then add the milk mixture and beaten egg. Add 1 cup of flour, the nuts, candied fruits and lemon rind. Mix well and add the remaining 2 cups of flour. Turn dough onto a lightly floured board and knead about 5 minutes. You may have to add more flour, but dough should be soft and smooth. Shape into a ball and place in an oiled bowl. Brush the top with oil and cover with a damp cloth. Let dough rise about an hour and a half or until doubled in bulk. Punch it down, cover and leave it alone for 5 to 10 minutes. Roll or press the dough into an oval about ½ inch thick or less. Spread half of it, lengthwise, with 1 tablespoon softened butter mixed with 2 tablespoons sugar and the cardamon. Fold the plain half over the other and place on a greased baking tin. Press the fold and ends down, cover and let rise again until doubled (about an hour or a little more).

Bake 30 to 35 minutes at 350 degrees.

For variation, you can add ½ cup of raisins, a little cinnamon, a tablespoon of brandy and it will still be real Stollen. But the plainer version seems to taste better for breakfast. Also, when the Stollen has cooled, it can be iced with confectioners' sugar mixed with a little water and lemon juice, and decorated with more candied fruits and nuts.

Date Bran Bread can be baked in loaves or muffin tins. This will make one loaf 8½ x 4½ inches or about twenty 2-inch muffins:

   1 cup dates, chopped
   1 cup boiling water
   1 egg
   ¼ cup dark molasses
   1 cup whole-grain flour
   1 teaspoon double-acting baking powder
   ½ teaspoon baking soda
   1 cup bran
   ½ teaspoon vanilla
   ½ cup walnuts, chopped

Pour the boiling water over the dates and let stand. In another bowl beat the egg strenuously and beat in the molasses thoroughly. Add to the egg mixture ½ cup of the flour, the baking powder and soda. Then add half the mixed dates and water, followed by the rest of the flour, the bran and vanilla. Add the remaining date mixture and the nuts last. Place batter in a greased loaf pan or muffin tins and bake about 1 hour at 350 degrees (less time for muffins, depending on their size).

CHAPTER THREE

The Indispensable Smithfield Ham

On the third day of Christmas my true love sent to me
Three French hens.

Indispensable because of its versatility: in its first triumphant appearance, impressively garnished and accompanied by tiny hot biscuits, it is the mainstay of a cocktail buffet or supper. Thin slices under plain creamed turkey or Eggs Goldenrod, or wrapped around asparagus, make a beautiful brunch or lunch. The rest is delicious for nibbling or in sandwiches; and the last crumbs are wonderful added to scrambled eggs, soups, vegetables or curries, or ground into a smooth, delectable spread.

If you are lucky enough to have some left and are temporarily bored with it, you can freeze it. Ham freezes very well if tightly wrapped: I have kept some as long as eight months with great success.

There are a few characters who presume to serve a whole Smithfield hot, and there are others (I among them) who consider this blasphemous. The flavor is best appreciated in tissue-thin slices, which are very hard to achieve until it has been thoroughly cooled.

The ham must be soaked for *hours*. About 2½ hours per pound seems to be the right ratio—24 or 25 hours for a ten-pounder, and more won't hurt it. Change the water three or four times.

The soaking container presents a problem because of the inclination of Virginia pigs to ranginess. I have used a wash boiler, a set laundry tub, and, in a particularly lush period, a garbage can kept for this purpose alone. If there is absolutely nothing large enough to hold it, saw off the hock, but get the ham completely covered. The next process, after soaking, is unpleasantly messy. The ham must be scrubbed, *hard*, with a stiff brush, until all the curing agents are removed; it should then be thoroughly rinsed.

Next, place the ham, skin down, in a boiler. A large covered roaster will do. The ham doesn't have to be entirely submerged if the pan is covered; though it does if the pan is uncovered, and the more liquid the better. Add a cup of brown sugar and a pint of cider. The cider is an optional maneuver. If there isn't any around the house, forget it; or substitute 5 or 6 green apples, quartered. Bring to a boil and simmer for 20 minutes to the pound or a little longer—about 3½ to 4 hours for a ten-pound ham. Add more water as necessary.

Let the ham stay in the cooking water until it is cool enough to handle but still warm. Take out of the water and remove the skin, using a very sharp knife. Scissors are helpful too. When the ham is cold, trim the fat to about ¼-inch thickness. If you feel compelled to gash the fat in diamonds and stud it with cloves, go ahead. But the classic way is to leave it alone. Sprinkle liberally with freshly ground black pepper, and then cover the ham with a *thick* layer of brown sugar.

Other coatings that are good are:

a paste made of prepared mustard, either hot or mild, brown sugar and sherry;

a mixture of black pepper, brown sugar, cracker crumbs and sherry;

orange marmalade and cracker crumbs.

Whatever you choose to do about the topping, the next step is to bake the ham at 400 degrees until it develops a rich brown glaze. This takes about a half hour or a little longer. Baste it first with a cup of sherry and later, at intervals of 10 minutes or so, baste with the drippings.

Let the ham cool at room temperature, then wrap it securely in wax paper or foil or plastic, and refrigerate until its debut as belle of the buffet.

CHAPTER FOUR

Wassail and Other Pleasures

On the fourth day of Christmas my true love sent to me
Four calling birds.

A good martini knows no season. Nor does a high-ball, nor anything on rocks. But at Christmas it is fun to add a few seasonal drinks to your repertory.

Wassail, as recorded in many recipes, varies in proportions as much as martinis do. One peculiar version makes a sort of apple-flavored Tom and Jerry, and another calls for 2 pounds of sugar to 1 quart of liquid. Typographical error, I hope! The recipe which follows will cheer 6 wassailers:

6 small tart apples
3 pints ale at room temperature
1 cup brown sugar
1 teaspoon each: ground ginger,
    cinnamon, nutmeg
2 or 3 whole cloves
thin strips of lemon peel from one lemon
1 pint Malaga wine or sherry

Core the apples and dry-roast them, without sugar, in a moderate oven until they almost burst and are white and fleecy. Combine 1 pint of the ale with the brown sugar, spices and lemon peel, and simmer for 10 or 15 minutes. Add the rest of the ale and wine, and heat thoroughly but do not boil.

A good way to serve wassail is to put an apple in each mug and ladle the hot spiced ale and wine over it. After several ladlings nearly everybody wants to eat the apple, now too soft to manage by hand, so provide spoons too.

Tom and Jerry, as produced by me, sometimes ends up as liquor-flavored scrambled eggs. The trick of making a successful one is supposed to be in the fast, mad stirring at the time of adding the hot water, and in using china or pottery mugs rather than metal. All I can say is, good luck! For 10 to 12 servings:

> *6 eggs*
> *1 cup powdered sugar*
> *¼ cup Jamaica rum*
> *1 ½ to 2 cups bourbon*
> *boiling water*
> *nutmeg*

Separate the whites and yolks of the eggs. Beat the whites stiff and gradually sift in the sugar. Beat the yolks thoroughly and then beat into the first mixture. Add the rum and bourbon. Cover and let stand 2 hours or more.

To serve, put 3 tablespoons of the egg mixture in a cup or mug and quickly stir in boiling water. Sprinkle with nutmeg.

Another way is to omit the bourbon in the egg mixture, pour it into the individual cups, add the hot water, and then, last of all, stir in the eggs.

Some versions add cinnamon and cloves to the egg mixture (about 1 teaspoon each); and some use hot milk instead of water

Buttered Rum, the delight of New England, packs quite a punch, especially if made with hard cider.

For each serving, place 2 ounces dark rum, a twist of lemon peel and a stick of cinnamon in a low tankard or mug. Fill with boiling cider or water, add a thin pat of butter and stir it with the cinnamon stick.

Vermont Punch is especially good as an after-winter-sports libation. A mixture of 2 parts whiskey, 2 parts lemon juice and 1 part maple syrup, served hot, makes a drink that is much better than it sounds.

Eggnogs can be thin, milky concoctions, or so thick that they must be eaten with a spoon. I like a medium texture, rich but drinkable. Most of the old "Colonial" recipes use only egg yolks (perhaps the whites went into a meringue or angel cake), and most of them use both whiskey and rum. For about 20 servings:

> *10 egg yolks*
> *½ pound confectioners' sugar*
> *2 pints spirits*
> *1 pint heavy cream, whipped*
> *nutmeg*
> *3 cups cold milk*

Beat the egg yolks until light. Add the sugar and beat until it is dissolved. Add the spirits slowly, while continuing to beat. (The spirits can be all rum, either light or dark; all bourbon; or part of each in any proportion that pleases you. I use 1½ pints bourbon to ½ pint dark rum.) Let this stand for 5 to 10 minutes; then add the milk and chill for a couple of hours. Just before serving, fold in the whipped cream and beat thoroughly. Serve in punch cups with a sprinkle of nutmeg.

Eggnog with Whole Eggs uses identical ingredients, plus egg whites, beaten stiff with a little salt and mixed in last, after the cream. This increases the volume, so it will make about 25 servings.

Peach Eggnog, a "sissy" type much admired by my grandmother, who couldn't have cared less about calories, uses for 12 servings:

>*6 egg yolks*
>*1 cup powdered sugar*
>*1 pint peach brandy*
>*1 cup cold milk*
>*1 pint heavy cream, whipped*
>*nutmeg*

The method of mixing is the same as in the first Eggnog recipe, but the end result is considerably thicker.

Champagne Punch is one of the easiest things to serve for festive occasions, and one of the most delicious versions I know of is the simplest to make. You can mix everything except the champagne ahead of time *or* have all the ingredients very cold and merely pour them over a large block of ice in the punch bowl. It works well either way, and calls for:

>*2 quarts apple juice (not cider)*
>*2 fifths light rum*
>*1 tablespoon Angostura bitters*
>*2 quarts champagne*

Whiskey Punch, which is a little more trouble, is made with:

>*3 lemons*
>*3 oranges*
>*2 cups granulated sugar*
>*3 cups hot, strong green tea*
>*1 pint brandy*
>*1 quart or more bourbon*

Grate the rinds of the lemons and oranges into a

large bowl. Add the sugar, the juice from the citrus fruits and the tea. Let this stand for half an hour or so, and add the brandy and bourbon. Chill and strain out the citrus peel. Taste. It may need a little dilution with water. This punch will keep practically forever if it is bottled and tightly corked.

Christmas Punch gets its color and flavor from cranberry juice and is milder than the preceding recipes. For about 28 to 30 punch-cup servings:

> *1 quart cranberry juice*
> *1 fifth sauterne*
> *½ pint brandy*
> *1 lemon, thinly sliced, unpeeled*
> *sugar to taste*
> *1 quart carbonated water*

Mix the juice, wine, brandy and lemon slices and let stand, covered, for a couple of hours. Now taste, and add sugar only if you really feel it is needed. Cranberry juice varies so much in sweetness that it may need none at all. Add the carbonated water just before serving. An especially attractive way to serve this punch is to freeze a large, fancy mold of more cranberry juice and use this instead of plain ice.

Bloody Marys seem to be as much a part of brunches as the food. Season tomato juice with lots of Worcestershire sauce, Tabasco, lemon or lime juice, celery salt, etc., to taste. Combine 2 parts of the spiced juice with 1 part vodka or gin. Shake well with cracked ice and serve in Whiskey Sour glasses or, on rocks, in Old Fashioned tumblers.

Bouillon, highly seasoned, combines well with bourbon, in the same 2 to 1 proportions, and cucumber peel is a good garnish.

Either of these is delicious served hot also.

Reindeer Milk was christened one heavy-headed morning when the whirring of the blender was almost unbearable. Its resuscitating powers are tremendous. Three or four hangovers can be mitigated with the following:

> ¼ *cup tomato catsup*
> *1 heaping tablespoon onion, chopped*
> ¼ *cup celery tops*
> *1 teaspoon Worcestershire sauce*
> *2 cups clam juice*
> *1 cup vodka*

Put the catsup, onion, celery tops and Worcestershire in a blender and purée. Add the clam juice gradually, with motor running at low speed. Then add the vodka and blend for a second or two. Pour over ice in an Old Fashioned glass and garnish with a lemon wedge.

Hot Chocolate On the nonalcoholic side, Christmas suggests steaming chocolate. Some of the best and richest is made in a blender. This makes 2 large cups and 2 dividend:

> *1 ½ squares unsweetened chocolate, cut in*
> *small pieces*
> ¼ *cup sugar*
> *pinch of salt*
> *2 cups hot milk*
> *whipped cream or marshmallows for garnish*

Blend the chocolate on high speed for 5 or 6 seconds. Turn mixer to low speed, add the rest of the ingredients and blend until frothy.

CHAPTER FIVE

Cocktail Buffets and Appetizers

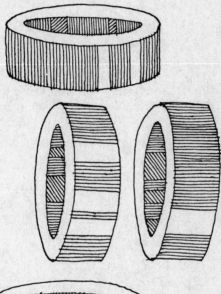

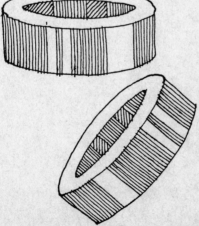

On the fifth day of Christmas my true love sent to me
Five gold rings.

Cocktail parties have a way of going on and on, and so the buffets should provide fairly substantial fare. Appetizers, on the other hand, should do just what the name suggests: they should complement the food to follow and should be served only in quantities sufficient to pique the appetite and not satiate it.

I like to "build" a cocktail buffet menu around one large main item, then choose other things for pleasantly contrasting appeal both in flavor and texture. The following menus have proved the principle valid.

Smithfield Ham

Tiny Hot Biscuits   Whipped Butter

Mustards

Pineapple Sticks   Melon Balls

Puffs with Chicken-Almond Filling

Dry-roasted Peanuts

Slice, paper-thin, as much of the ham (page 23) as you think will be consumed, and group the slices around the rest of the ham on a large platter. Garnish it with plenty of parsley and crisp radish roses. The biscuits should be very small and very hot, capable of melting the butter on contact. A choice of two or three mustards would be thoughtful; and the pineapple sticks and melon balls impaled on picks add a refreshing touch. The Puffs (page 43) filled with Chicken-Almond Spread (page 39) and the dry-roasted peanuts blend beautifully with the ham.

The second menu is somewhat heartier.

Cold Roast Beef

Horseradish Sauce   Chutney-A1 Sauce

Small Hot Rolls   Whipped Butter

Onion Brochettes

Canapés of Liver Pâté on Black Bread

Apple Wedges

Blue Cheese

For the cold roast beef a fillet, a rib eye, and a sirloin tip all work equally well. Roast the beef rare. Chill well before carving and garnish attractively with greenery. Both Horseradish Sauce (page 42) and Chutney-A1 (page 41) are nice served with it.

Onion Brochettes complement the beef. On small skewers alternate squares of green pepper with very small parboiled white onions (use 2 of each). Finish with a canned mushroom cap. Brush them with melted butter and broil 4 to 5 minutes.

Liver Pâté (page 37) spread on tissue-thin black bread cut in gay shapes is another good accompaniment. And a tray of crisp, unpeeled apple wedges with a good blue cheese is colorful and delicious. Roll the apples in lemon juice to prevent discoloration.

The third menu was originally intended for Friday, but turned out to be so good that it has been repeated on other days.

Sea Food Assortment
Stuffed Eggs   Stuffed Jalopena Peppers
Garlic Sauce
Cucumber-Anchovy Canapés
Hot Shoestring Potatoes

Make a bed of cracked ice on a tremendous tray and arrange on it an assortment of sea food: shrimp, lobster chunks, crab claws, clams, whatever is currently available. Garnish the tray with stuffed eggs and canned Mexican Jalopena Peppers stuffed with cheese. Serve Garlic Sauce (page 41) and keep it hot over a spirit lamp or Sterno burner. Cucumber-Anchovy Canapés (page 39) are a bland contrast. And bowls of hot shoestring potatoes add crispness.

This fourth menu is quite substantial, and since

very few of the foods can be managed with fingers, small plates and forks are essential.

Lasagne

Antipasto

Ring of Artichoke Hearts and Avocado

Ratatouille

Italian Bread

It's a good idea to divide the total amount of Lasagne (page 117) into two, or even three, baking dishes, serving one at a time. Smaller ones, fresh from a warm oven, are more appealing than one large one that looks "used" after the first foray.

There is so much cheese in the Lasagne that I wouldn't include any more in the Antipasto, but almost anything else will do: anchovies or sardines; cherry tomatoes, either plain or stuffed with little rolls of smoked salmon; olives (especially garlic olives); slices of salami or pepperoni; and celery hearts and radishes for crispness. A jellied ring of Artichoke Hearts and Avocado (page 105) would be good, as well as chilled Ratatouille (page 118) and crusty bread.

Most of the following appetizer and canapé mainstays can be made ahead of time, and some of them can be frozen. Spreads made with cream cheese can be frozen but should not be stored frozen more than 2 weeks. Spreads "bound" with condensed soup will keep as long as a month. But don't freeze any that contain large quantities of fresh vegetables.

Baked Liver Pâté is a fine place to begin:

2 pounds raw pork liver

1 ½ pounds pork suet

1 cup chopped onion

2 cloves garlic, peeled

1 bay leaf

1 heaping tablespoon salt
⅛ teaspoon each: cloves, thyme, nutmeg
½ teaspoon black pepper
salt pork
mushroom slices

Remove skin and membrane from the liver. Grind together the liver, suet, onion, garlic and bay leaf. Use the finest blade; and put them through the grinder at least three times, more if you see any lumps. Mix in the spices and pack tightly in a buttered glass loaf pan. The mixture will be quite soupy. Cover the top with thin slices of salt pork and bake 1½ hours at 350 degrees. Remove the salt pork. Chill, unmold, garnish and serve very cold. Very thin lengthwise slices of mushrooms, raw or cooked, make an attractive garnish.

Jellied Liver Pâté

1 pound chicken livers
½ cup onion, chopped
1 clove garlic, peeled
½ bay leaf
2 cups chicken broth
1 hard-boiled egg
¼ pound butter
1 teaspoon anchovy paste
salt and pepper to taste
1 tablespoon gelatin
½ cup sherry

Simmer together for about 10 minutes the livers, onion, garlic, bay leaf and broth. Strain, reserving the broth; put all the solids and 1 cup of the liquid in a blender. Add the boiled egg, butter and seasonings and purée until smooth. In a fairly large bowl, soften the gelatin in the sherry. Heat the other cup of broth to boiling and add to the gelatin, stirring until it is dissolved. Then add the blender contents and mix thoroughly. Pour into an oiled mold or loaf pan and chill 6 to 8 hours.

Liver Spread The rather indifferent product offered by most meat packers can be made a lot more interesting by adding to one 3-ounce can, one cooked, mashed chicken liver, 2 tablespoons butter, 1 tablespoon brandy and a little salt. Mix smooth and chill.

Smithfield Spread is made by dumping into a blender:

> *½ cup condensed cream of mushroom soup*
> *1 cup ham crumbs*
> *½ cup unsalted peanuts*
> *2 tablespoons onion, chopped*
> *½ teaspoon dry mustard*

Purée until smooth. You can make this spread with mild smoked ham too; in which case add salt or use salted peanuts and a little more mustard.

Chicken-Almond Spread is made the same way, using chicken instead of ham, and almonds instead of peanuts; no mustard, but salt and pepper to taste. This is also a good filling for tiny Puffs (page 43).

Cucumber-Anchovy Spread Peel and remove the seeds from cucumber. Coarsely grate the cucumber meat and plunge in ice water for 30 minutes. Drain and pat dry on towels. To one part cucumber add ¼ part chopped anchovy fillets, and bind with mayonnaise.

Christmas Cabbage should be spread on thin rye bread or pumpernickel; fancy shapes add to the appeal.

> *1 cup raw red cabbage*
> *½ cup raw green pepper*
> *¼ cup blue cheese*

Chop all ingredients very fine and bind with mayonnaise or thick sour cream.

Cheddar-Chutney is intended to be served hot. Either spread on toast and place in a hot oven until the cheese melts, or fill Puffs (page 43) and heat for 10 minutes or so. The filled puffs may be frozen and will keep in the freezer about a month; give the frozen puffs a little more time in the oven when reheating them.

> *½ cup mango chutney, chopped*
> *1 cup coarsely grated cheddar cheese*

Bind with condensed cheese soup.

Red Caviar Spread   Serve in a bowl, with canapé cases and a spoon for filling them.

> *1 3-ounce package cream cheese*
> *1 cup sour cream*
> *1 teaspoon onion, grated*
> *1 teaspoon lemon juice*
> *1 4-ounce jar red caviar*

Mix together, adding the caviar last gently to avoid smashing the roe.

Red Caviar Dip is the same thing without the cream cheese and with stronger seasoning of Tabasco and/or Worcestershire sauce. This dip and raw cucumber sticks have a special affinity for each other; also lengthwise center slices of large raw mushrooms.

Hot Garlic Dip is used for vegetables and sea food. Try peeled broccoli stems as well as the more usual raw cauliflower, celery and carrots.

>*4 cloves garlic, peeled, sliced*
>*¼ cup butter*
>*¼ cup olive oil*
>*1 cup heavy cream*
>*salt or soy sauce to taste*

Place the garlic, butter and olive oil in a small saucepan and sauté for 4 or 5 minutes. Remove the garlic and add the cream and salt. Heat and keep hot while serving.

Hot Anchovy Dip is identical, except for the addition of 6 to 8 mashed anchovy fillets.

Hot Curry Dip is much the same. Prepare Garlic Dip and cook 1 tablespoon curry powder with the garlic. This is hot in flavor as well as temperature, so you may prefer to use less curry.

Chutney-A1 Sauce is especially good with beef, but seems to enhance all meats.

Boil together for 10 minutes 1 cup of mango chutney and 1 bottle (5¼ ounces) of A1 sauce. Strain and rebottle.

Horseradish Sauce is also good with beef and can be used as a shellfish dip too.

> *1 cup sour cream*
> *1 cup canned strained apple sauce*
> *½ cup prepared hot horseradish*

Combine well and chill. A little tomato catsup may be added, mostly for color.

Mushroom Caps of medium size make lovely cases for a variety of fillings. Remove the stems and dip the mushroom caps in melted butter or olive oil; pile the filling high in the center of the caps and bake on an oiled tin about 15 minutes at 350 degrees.

NUT FILLING is made by chopping the mushroom stems very fine and sautéing them in butter for 3 or 4 minutes. Add finely chopped nuts (pecans, walnuts, etc.) in quantity equal to the mushroom stems. Then add fine dry bread crumbs in equal bulk (½ cup stems, ½ cup nuts, 1 cup crumbs). Season with chopped chives, salt, pepper and basil and moisten with a little cream or sherry. Fill the mushroom caps, dot with butter and bake.

SAUSAGE MEAT cooked with chopped apple and onion and bound with bread crumbs is another good filling.

Or try various spreads (liver, ham, etc.), or put a smoked oyster in each cap, add a dash of hot pepper sauce, mask it with mayonnaise or sour cream and bake.

Bacon-Wrapped Titbits are easily constructed ahead of time. Almost anything bite-sized can be bacon-wrapped successfully: sautéed chicken livers, oysters either smoked or raw, stuffed olives, chunks of fruit such as bananas or pineapple.

I have found that the titbits are more easily managed if the bacon is first cooked on one side until just limp. Drain it, and when it is cool enough to handle, wrap the titbits, placing the cooked side of the bacon next to the food, the uncooked side outside. Fasten the bacon with picks. Use a rack in a shallow pan so that all the grease will drain off; broil or bake in a hot oven until the bacon is crisp.

Puffs are usable for many things. As an appetizer, they should be baked very small. Use a demitasse spoon to shape them. Fill with a spread or finely minced salad and serve either heated or at room temperature, depending on the filling.

The baked puffs, without filling, can be frozen and will keep a couple of months. Thaw in a slow oven and let them crisp slightly before filling. This will make 50 to 60 puffs.

> *1 cup water*
> *½ cup butter*
> *½ teaspoon salt*
> *1 cup flour*
> *4 to 5 whole eggs, at room temperature*

Put the water, butter and salt in a heavy saucepan. When the butter melts and the mixture boils, add the flour all at once. Stir *rapidly* until the paste leaves the sides of the pan and forms a ball. Remove the pan from the heat and cool 2 or 3 minutes. Add the eggs, 1 at a time, beating briskly after each addition. If a small bit of paste will stand erect when scooped up on a spoon, the paste is ready to bake. Depending on the size of the eggs, this might happen after the fourth one has been added. Drop the paste by spoonfuls, about an inch apart, on a buttered cookie sheet. Shape and bake 10 minutes at 400 degrees; then reduce the heat to 350 degrees and bake 20 to 25 minutes longer. Cool before filling or wrapping to store.

Cheese Pastry can be assembled in many flavors, shapes and sizes. The basic pastry is made with:

> ½ *pound cream cheese* or
> *1 cup "American" cheese, shredded* or
> > *1 cup blue cheese, crumbled*
> ½ *pound butter*
> *2 cups flour, sifted*
> *1 teaspoon salt*

Have cheese and butter at room temperature and mix them well together. Add the flour and salt and work together with hands until the dough is firm. Chill 3 hours or more. Roll the dough ⅓ inch thick, cut and bake on a floured pan at 425 degrees for about 10 minutes for flat cookies, a little longer for rolled.

Caraway and sesame seeds are very good with all the cheese flavors. Sprinkle on top of cut cookies; or sprinkle on flat dough, roll into a pinwheel, slice and bake.

Or make very small tart shells. After baking them, fill, for example, with a dab of red caviar and sour cream or with creamed mushrooms.

Or wrap dough around small cooked sausages and bake.

Dynamite Sticks are American cheese pastry cut in thin strips, 2 to 3 inches long and liberally doused with cayenne pepper.

In serving any canapé, keep the garnish simple but appropriate. Use just enough to enhance its appearance and not interfere with the primary flavor. Tiny sprigs of parsley, sliced olives, capers, chopped or sliced egg, chopped chives, small leaves cut from thin cucumber peel, "flowers" of beets, carrots or turnips are some suggestions.

Happy Cocktails!

CHAPTER SIX

The Last Fast of Advent

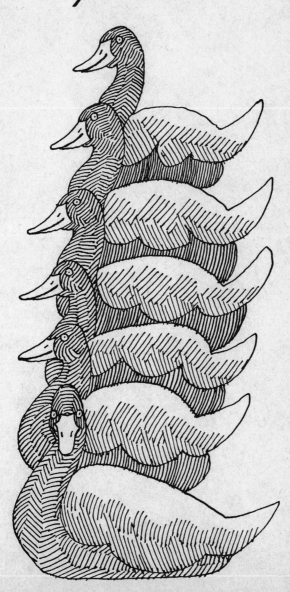

On the sixth day of Christmas my true love sent to me
Six geese a-laying.

The fast of Advent is traditionally climaxed with a magnificent fish dinner on Christmas Eve. The menu might go like this:

Eggs Nicholas   Christmas Cabbage Canapés
"Christmas Carp" with Wine-Cream Sauce
Ring of Shoestring Beets   Parsleyed Potato Balls
Sesame Biscuits
Butter
Sauterne or Riesling
Coffee Chiffon Pie
Coffee

A whole baked fish is, by far, the most impressive main course for Christmas Eve. It is also the most trouble, requiring somebody's presence in the kitchen for an hour or more before serving. It must be watched over tenderly, basted frequently, and a sauce must be made for it, etc.

As a prelude, with drinks, the **Eggs Nicholas** are delicious. These are ordinary stuffed eggs with a generous topping of black caviar. The Christmas Cabbage Canapés (page 40) provide a crunchy contrast.

Whole Baked Fish   Carp is a traditional Christmas fish, but almost any kind of whole, fairly fat fish will do. To serve six, buy a four- or five-pound fish, scaled and cleaned but with head and tail intact. If the fish market will remove the backbone, have it removed, but you can do it by cutting with a *sharp* knife, on each side of the bone, approaching from the cavity. Snip the bone at head and tail ends with poultry shears and pull the bone out. You can also remove the dorsal fin, if you want to, by cutting down close to it on either side for its full length, and giving it a quick jerk toward the head. Some of the attached bones will come out with it, and the more bones you can do away with, the easier the fish will be to serve. Wash the cavity and stuff it. Skewer or sew the sides together. You will need about 2 cups of stuffing for a five-pound fish. Here again almost any kind will do, but one that is especially good is made of:

> *¼ cup each: chopped celery, chopped*
> *onion, chopped almonds*
> *2 tablespoons butter*
> *1 ½ cups soft bread crumbs*
> *salt, pepper and basil to taste*
> *white wine*

Sauté the celery, onion and almonds in the butter until onions are limp but not brown. Add the bread crumbs and seasonings and enough wine to moisten the mixture.

Another one, made the same way, omits the almonds and substitutes crumbled corn bread for the bread crumbs. Chopped mushrooms or oysters or shrimp can be added too with delicious effect. If you want a firmer stuffing, add a well-beaten egg.

Oil a shallow baking pan that is large enough to hold the fish in a peacefully prone position. (I once baked a whole fish in a large ring mold with repulsive results. It stared at us balefully while seeming to swim off the platter.)

Tear off a sheet of aluminum foil long enough to put under the fish lengthwise, with ends extending 6 or 8 inches. Fold it in thirds lengthwise, put it in the pan and lay the fish on top. This will help lift the cooked fish to its serving platter.

Take 6 or 7 strips of bacon and crisscross them diagonally across the fish, tucking the ends under.

Place in a 425-degree oven for 10 minutes. Then reduce the heat to 350 degrees and baste.

The basting liquid, which also serves as the base

for the accompanying sauce, is made by boiling together for 10 minutes:

> *1 cup onion, chopped*
> *1 cup celery. chopped*
> *1 tablespoon lemon peel, grated*
> *1 teaspoon salt*
> *½ teaspoon pepper*
> *3 cups dry white wine*
> *1 bay leaf*

Reduce the heat and allow to barely simmer.

Baste madly, every 10 minutes or so. Allow 12 minutes cooking time per pound—an hour for a five-pound fish (but test it with a fork after 45 minutes: it may be done, depending on the variety of fish).

When it *is* done, lift it carefully to its serving platter, and remove the skewers or thread. Keep the fish warm by wrapping the lifting foil over it and returning it to the oven with the heat off.

If the bacon has become crisp and attractive, leave it on; otherwise remove it.

If there is more than 2 tablespoons of bacon fat in the pan, skim off the excess. Add the remaining basting liquid to the pan. There should be about a cupful or a little more. Bring this to a boil, stirring; then reduce the heat and blend in 1 cup of sour cream. Add a few drops of Tabasco sauce, taste and "correct the seasoning" and heat thoroughly but do not boil. Strain into a serving dish and keep warm.

Wreathe the fish in greenery—parsley, water cress, celery leaves or whatever. Decorate with a few thin slices of lemon. Also provide, in the garnish or separately, some good-sized squeezable lemon wedges.

The shoestring beets can be freshly made or frozen or canned. Serve them in a ring on a round platter and fill the center with tiny potato balls smothered in parsley butter.

For the biscuits, make your own or use ready-to-bake ones. Before putting them in the oven, brush the tops with melted butter and dip in sesame seeds.

The Coffee Chiffon Pie (page 119) is light but satisfying. And make the beverage strong and plentiful: you will probably be up for hours and need more of it.

Here is another menu, not so demanding of last-minute attention:

Red Caviar Dip (page 40)
Cucumber Sticks   Thin-sliced Pumpernickel
Lobster Tails with Wild Rice
Shrimp Sauce
Tomatoes Parmesan   Brussels Sprouts
Hard Crusty Rolls or French Bread
Butter
Lemon Sherbet
Hot Mincemeat Puffs
Coffee

Lobster Tails with Wild Rice For 6 servings:

2 tablespoons butter
½ cup carrot, chopped
½ cup celery, chopped
1 cup green onions with tops, chopped
4 cups water
2 vegetable bouillon cubes
½ teaspoon salt
1 ½ cups wild rice
6 frozen lobster tails

Wash the wild rice and soak it if recommended by the packer. (Some brands are pre-soaked.)

Melt the butter in a saucepan or electric skillet. Add the carrot, celery and green onions and sauté 3 or 4 minutes. Now add the water, bouillon cubes, salt and drained rice. Bring to a boil and simmer, covered, until rice is tender and water is absorbed (about 40 minutes). Add more water if needed.

Boil the lobster tails as directed on the package. Cut in ¼-inch slices and add to the cooked rice. All this can be done a day ahead of time.

Shrimp Sauce
2 10½-ounce cans frozen cream of shrimp soup
½ cup sherry
¼ cup butter
pepper and Tabasco sauce to taste
salt if needed (the soup is quite salty)

Mix all the ingredients together in a double boiler and heat thoroughly. If sauce seems too thick, add more sherry.

Mix ⅔ of the sauce with the rice and lobster, and put it into a shallow buttered casserole (2 to 2½ quarts) or a deep, ovenproof platter. Arrange 12 (or more) thick slices of tomato around the edges. Top tomatoes with a mixture of equal parts dry bread crumbs and parmesan cheese. Dot with butter and bake 30 minutes at 375 degrees. Serve the remaining sauce separately.

Make a "production" of grocery-store sherbet by packing it into a melon mold several hours before serving. Unmold and garnish with small clumps of holly: maraschino cherries for the berries and leaves cut from large green gum drops.

Fill tiny Puff cases (page 43) with Mincemeat (page 10) and put them in a very slow oven (200 degrees or so) when the first part of dinner is served.

Not everyone is shivering in ice and snow at Christmas time; and for those who are lucky enough to be in a milder climate, the following menu featuring fish steaks in aspic is suggested.

Red Caviar Spread (page 40)   Canapé Cases
Salmon-glazed Fish Steaks
Asparagus, Tomatoes and Water Cress
Sauce Mousseline
Cheese Soufflé
Mexican Christmas Eve Salad (Altered Version)

Salmon-Glazed Fish Steaks For 6 servings, buy 6 fish steaks cut about 1 inch thick. Fresh or frozen salmon is wonderful if you can get it, but I have also used kingfish with good results. You will need:

1 quart water
1 small onion, stuck with 2 or 3 cloves
3 thin slices lemon
3 or 4 peppercorns
2 leafy tops of celery
1 ½ teaspoons salt
1 tablespoon unflavored gelatin
½ cup dry white wine
¼ pound smoked salmon
garnishes for aspic: olives, truffle, etc.

Make a court bouillon by simmering together the first six ingredients for 15 minutes.

Place the fish steaks in a large skillet and poach them in the strained court bouillon "until done" (when the flesh is no longer translucent and flakes easily). Timing depends on the variety of fish. Remove the steaks carefully to an oiled rimmed cookie sheet of a size that will fit in the refrigerator. Skin the fish and chill thoroughly.

Strain the court bouillon again to remove any bits

of fish and allow it to cool. Soften the gelatin in the wine in the top of a double boiler and then dissolve it over hot water. Remove from the hot water and add 1½ cups of the cooled bouillon. Chill this until it is slightly thickened.

Purée the smoked salmon in a blender. Mix it with ½ cup of the thickened aspic and mask the fish with this. At this point set whatever garnish you want in the purée on top of the steaks. Sliced olives are attractive, or bits of pimento. Thin slices of truffle are classic, but at four dollars a very tiny tin they are hardly worth it. Chill again until set; then spoon the rest of the aspic over the steaks, letting it drip down into the pan. You may have to warm the aspic a little if it has become too firm. The fish should be smoothly coated about ⅛ inch thick above the purée. Chill again until it is all very firm.

To serve, lift the steaks onto a large, cold platter. Dice fine all the aspic in the pan and arrange it around the fish. Asparagus spears, cooked and chilled, tomato quarters and water cress (or parsley) garnish the platter. Use enough asparagus to "count" as a vegetable and serve with Sauce Mousseline (page 76) or plain sour cream.

Cheese Soufflé can double as bread. I suggest providing butter and small separate plates for it so that it doesn't get mixed up with melting fish aspic.

> ½ *cup butter*
> ½ *cup flour*
> 2 *cups milk*
> 2 *cups cheddar cheese, coarsely grated*
> 8 *egg yolks*
> 10 *egg whites, beaten stiff*
> *salt and pepper to taste*

In the top of a double boiler over direct medium heat melt the butter and stir in the flour. Add the milk and seasonings and blend smooth. Remove the pan from the heat and add the egg yolks, beating in one at a time alternately with the cheese. Put the pan over hot water and stir until the cheese has melted and the mixture is medium thick. Now cool the mixture for 5 minutes or so and then fold in the beaten egg whites. Pour into a buttered 3-quart soufflé dish and bake at 375 degrees for about 40 minutes or a little less. The soufflé should be moist in the center. Serve this *at once*. There is *no* time for an extra drink after you have taken the soufflé out of the oven.

Mexican Christmas Eve Salad In the original salad, beets are a prominent ingredient. But they are not too appropriate when the salad is serving as a substitute for dessert. Actually this altered version is just a beautifully mixed-up assortment of fruit, topped with pomegranate seeds and chopped peanuts. Fresh fruit is preferable, but frozen or even canned may be used too. Serve very thin mayonnaise with it, if you like, but usually only sugar is added. The following combination is a good one and is authentic (except for the omission of 1 cup of cooked sliced beets). For 6 servings:

> 1 ½ *cups pineapple chunks*
> 1 *cup apples, unpeeled, but cored and thinly*
>   *sliced lengthwise*
> 1 ½ *cups orange sections, peeled*
> ½ *cup sliced bananas*
> *seeds from 1 fresh pomegranate*
> ½ *cup unsalted peanuts, coarsely chopped*

The above ingredients are basic. You can add any other fruits that suit you. One I particularly like is preserved guava shells, cut in thin strips (about ¼ cup of strips for the above quantities).

The simplest of all menus for Christmas Eve features:

Shrimp and Oyster Gumbo
Rice
Corn Sticks   Butter
Della Robbia Wine

Serve Dynamite Sticks (page 44) with drinks first and then the gumbo, in a tureen, to be spooned into large soup plates over fluffy white rice. The corn sticks blend well with the gumbo, and Della Robbia Wine is a refreshing dessert.

Shrimp and Oyster Gumbo Almost everybody has a favorite gumbo recipe. The following, which makes about 4 quarts, is authentic Louisiana:

⅛ *pound diced salt pork*
1 heaping tablespoon flour
1 cup onion, chopped
1 pound raw okra, thinly sliced, or
 2 10-ounce packages frozen okra
2 quarts hot water
1 pint oysters, with their liquor
1 small hot red pepper
1 bay leaf
¼ *cup celery leaves, minced*
salt to taste
*1 tablespoon Filé powder**
1 cup tomatoes, peeled, chopped
2 pounds raw shrimp, shelled, deveined
¼ *cup parsley, chopped*

*Filé powder is seldom used in an authentic gumbo containing okra, but it adds a great deal to the flavor.

Fry the salt pork in a large heavy saucepan or

Dutch oven. Remove the crisp pork pieces and reserve. Add the flour and brown it lightly. Put in the onion and half the okra. Cook for 3 or 4 minutes, stirring constantly (the okra tends to burn). Add the water and liquor from the oysters, the seasonings and tomatoes. If you use the Filé powder, add it at this point. Cover and simmer slowly for 40 minutes. Add the raw shrimp and cook 20 minutes longer.

Turn the heat down *very* low and add the oysters, the rest of the sliced okra and the parsley. Simmer for 15 or 20 minutes. Just before serving, add the crisp bits of pork. (Omit if strict fasting is essential.)

Della Robbia Wine Pour port or medium-sweet sherry into small low glasses centered on dessert plates. Surround the wine with fruit in bite-sized pieces: pineapple, melon balls, figs, mandarin orange sections, etc. The fruit is dipped in the wine before it is eaten (with oyster or salad forks) and the remaining wine is sipped.

CHAPTER SEVEN

The First Feast of Christmas

On the seventh day of Christmas my true love sent to me
Seven swans a-swimming.

7. The First Feast of Christmas

After Mass on Christmas Eve, when Christmas itself at last has arrived, a joyful gathering to celebrate the event is a very pleasant custom.

The late hour deters some people, and probably the whole idea should be skipped by parents of tiny children with prospects of early rising, or by those who have a busy schedule on Christmas Day and a huge dinner to prepare. But all of the menus suggested can be used on other occasions. A most beautiful late supper could consist of:

Oysters on the Half Shell

Pork Sausages

Marinaded Artichoke Hearts   Red Pepper Strips

Liver Pâté

Quiche

Fruitcake

Champagne or Champagne Punch

The oysters, reposing on a large tray of cracked ice, should be well seasoned with lemon juice, Tabasco, salt and pepper. The marinaded artichokes and sweet red pepper strips decorate the ice-filled tray. A dish of tiny pork sausages goes alongside the tray. (Eat an oyster first, followed by a hot sausage.) Serve the chilled Liver Pâté (page 37) in thin slices and the warm, creamy Quiche in wedges. Fruitcake (pages 7 and 8) provides something sweet and Champagne or Champagne Punch (page 30) something festive.

Small plates and forks are the only utensils needed, plus glasses or punch cups; so, although the supper is elaborate in appearance, the service is simple.

Quiche There are many controversial recipes for Quiche. Some require precooking of the custard in a double boiler before baking in the pie shell. Some ignore this and demand that flour and melted butter be added. If onions are added, the Quiche changes boundaries and becomes "Alsacienne" instead of "Lorraine." The following recipe has been successful:

pastry for a one-crust 9-inch pie
1 egg white
6 to 8 strips of bacon
½ pound Swiss cheese cut in thin strips
2 cups light cream
4 eggs
1 tablespoon flour
½ teaspoon nutmeg
½ teaspoon salt
dash of cayenne pepper
1 ½ tablespoons melted butter

Line a 9-inch pie plate with the pastry. Prick it all over with a fork, brush with egg white and bake 5 minutes at 450 degrees. Cool.

Fry the bacon crisp, drain it well and crumble. Put into the pie shell together with the cheese.

Scald the cream and cool slightly.

In a bowl beat together the eggs, flour and seasonings. Add the cream and melted butter and mix well. Pour the custard over the cheese and bacon and bake for 35 to 40 minutes at 375 degrees until the custard is set and lightly browned. Since Quiche should be served warm, not hot, allow 10 or 15 minutes for it to rest quietly after baking.

A Chili supper is always welcome late in the evening.

Chili
Tortillas   *Crackers*   *Black Bread*
Mild Cheese
Red Onion Rings
Beer

Chili This is a Texas type which will make 10 to 12 generous servings:

> 2 cloves garlic, minced
> 1 cup onion, chopped
> 3 tablespoons olive oil
> 2 pounds lean beef, chopped
> 4 cups canned tomatoes, undrained or
>   4 cups beef stock or bouillon
> 2 teaspoons salt
> 1 bay leaf
> 1 teaspoon oregano
> ¼ teaspoon crushed cumin
> 2 to 3 tablespoons chili powder
> 2 16-ounce cans red chili beans, undrained

Use a deep heavy kettle or Dutch oven, and cook the garlic, onion, olive oil and beef together for about 10 minutes. The meat should be chopped, not ground, and cooked, at this stage, only long enough to lose its red color. Next add the tomatoes *or* beef stock. (I like tomatoes, but there are purists who deplore them.) Add the seasonings and simmer for about an hour or until meat is very tender. Then add the chili beans and simmer for another 30 minutes.

Make this a day or two ahead if you can, for it gets better with age. It can also be made weeks ahead of time and frozen. Freeze only the meat mixture and add the beans when reheating.

Note on easier preparation: If a *really* good chili can be bought in your locality, what are you waiting for?

Eggs are always with us, and besides the impromptu scrambled or fried, with bacon or whatever happens to be in the refrigerator, you might try this menu:

Curried Eggs and Sausage
Rice
Chopped Green Pepper   *Chinese Noodles*
Chutney
Beer

Curried Eggs and Sausage   For 6 servings:

10 or 12 hard-cooked eggs
1 pound bulk sausage
1 cup fine bread crumbs
1 beaten egg
1 cup onion, chopped
3 teaspoons curry powder
3 tablespoons flour
2 cups chicken broth
1 cup light cream

Peel the eggs and cut them in quarters or thick slices. Mix the sausage and bread crumbs with the beaten egg. Form into marble-sized balls and cook them in an electric or heavy iron frying pan. Remove from the pan and cook the onion in ⅓ cup of the sausage drippings for 3 or 4 minutes. Then add the curry powder and flour and cook 3 or 4 minutes more. Gradually add the chicken broth and cream. Blend the mixture well and simmer until thickened, stirring often. Then add the eggs and sausage balls and heat thoroughly. A sprinkling of chopped parsley improves the appearance.

Small separate bowls of green pepper and noodles to sprinkle on the eggs will provide a crisp note to round out this repast. And the chutney and beer complement the curry.

For a small group of four or five, something in a chafing dish is easy and pleasantly accomplished. A Welsh Rabbit (or Rarebit—the sources seem equally divided on this long-standing debate) is wonderful if you can do it. (Mine have always been stringy. But there is really delicious prepared Rabbit that needs only heating.) Served on freshly made toast or on a slice of grilled tomato, or both, it is a satisfying before-bed snack.

Creamed Chipped Beef and Mushrooms is a little more trouble, but worth it. The following makes 4 generous servings or 6 modest ones:

> ½ pound dried beef
> ½ pound fresh mushrooms, sliced
> 5 tablespoons butter
> 3 tablespoons flour
> 2 cups milk
> salt (be careful, the beef is very salty)
> pepper
> Worcestershire Sauce
> 2 tablespoons green pepper, diced
> chopped chives

Cut the beef in thin strips with scissors. Place it in a strainer; run hot water through it and dry well on paper towels.

Melt the butter in the top pan of the chafing dish over direct flame. Add the beef and mushrooms and cook slowly for 4 or 5 minutes. Sprinkle the flour into the pan and blend out any lumps. Add the milk slowly, stirring constantly, and cook until it is thick and smooth. Place the top pan over the hot-water pan and add the seasonings to taste and green pepper. Cover the pan and cook about 5 minutes. (Don't overcook or the pepper will lose its crispness.)

Toasted frozen waffles make a good base for this, and a sprinkling of chopped chives is both colorful and delicious.

If you are making this before an audience, have all the ingredients, measured and ready to assemble, grouped around the chafing dish in an attractive arrangement. However, it will "hold" over a very low flame for quite a long time. I have made it just before going to Midnight Mass and, on returning, found the meal in excellent shape.

CHAPTER EIGHT

Christmas Dinner

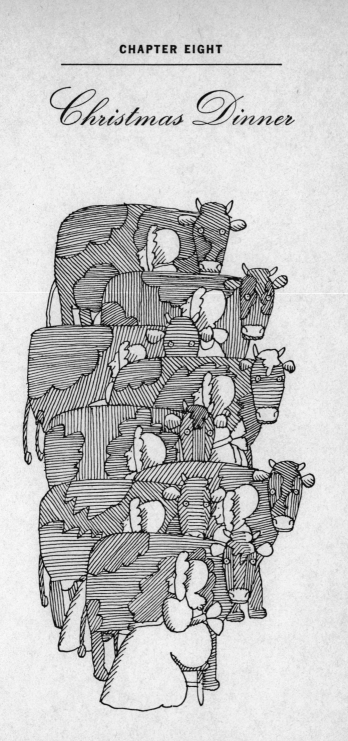

On the eighth day of Christmas my true love sent to me
Eight maids a-milking.

The festive board should provide a memorable feast for both palate and eye, and the following "Partridge in a Pear Tree" is one to be remembered with great pleasure.

Ham-stuffed Mushrooms
Celery and Carrot Curls
Partridge in a Pear Tree
Rice with Currants
Gravy
Souffléd Squash   String Beans with Almonds
Chocolate-Chestnut Mold
Rosé Wine

The Ham-stuffed Mushrooms (page 42) and celery and carrot curls accompany drinks first. They are followed by the "partridges," which are grouse or large-sized Cornish hens. They are stuffed with rice and currants and roasted with lavish bastings of butter and rosé wine. More rice is placed in the middle of a very large oval platter and the birds are nested on it, heading diagonally, in opposite directions. "Tree" branches of celery tops are made at both ends of the platter, and placed among these are halves of preserved pears, the centers filled with currant jelly.

Served with this are Gravy and Souffléd Squash and String Beans with Almonds. For dessert, a Chocolate-Chestnut Mold with whipped cream. A refreshing, chilled rosé is served throughout the meal.

Partridge (In this country it would be more authentic to call it grouse.) If your personal Nimrod has provided some, cook them this way:

Allow about a pound of bird per person. If you prefer not to stuff game birds, just wipe them and put a small peeled onion and a little salt and pepper in each one. Otherwise stuff them with the Rice and Currant mixture (page 71). Wrap them with bacon or salt pork, securing it with string. Put them into a 450-degree oven; while roasting, baste frequently, first with a cup of rosé and then with drippings. Cook for about 15 minutes and test for doneness. The meat should be pink, and some people prefer it really rare, so be sure to allow for the subsequent browning time. The cooking time depends, of course, on the size of the birds. If they are fairly large, they may take another 15 minutes. When the moment has arrived, remove the bacon or salt pork, roll the birds around in the pan drippings and dust the breasts with fine bread crumbs. Put them in another baking pan and return to the oven to brown.

GRAVY Have the livers ready, sautéed or boiled and then minced.

> ¼ *cup fat from roasting pan*
> *1 ½ cups chicken stock*
> ½ *cup rosé wine*
> *2 tablespoons flour*
> ¼ *cup currant jelly*
> *salt and pepper to taste*
> *minced livers*

Pour off all the fat remaining in the roasting pan and heat ¼ cup of it in a saucepan. Then add the chicken stock and wine to the roasting pan. Set over very low heat on top of the stove and scrape the pan well, deglazing it thoroughly. Let this simmer while you blend the flour with the heated fat and cook it 3 or 4 minutes. Strain the liquid from the roasting pan into the roux and stir until smooth. Add the jelly, seasonings and livers and stir until the jelly melts.

Cornish Hens can be stuffed and roasted like chickens. As they are fatter than grouse, they don't need to be larded; but rub the breasts and legs with butter. Preheat the oven to 450 degrees and reduce the heat to 350 degrees as soon as the birds are put in. Allow about 20 minutes per pound. In roasting two or more birds, don't count the total weight, just the individual size. Baste them with ½ cup butter melted in ½ cup rosé, and make gravy in the same way as for the grouse.

Rice with Currants can be made a day ahead of time.

> *3 cups raw rice*
> *6 to 7 cups chicken broth*
> *½ cup butter*
> *1 cup onion, chopped*
> *1 cup celery, chopped*
> *1 cup currants*
> *¼ cup rosé wine*
> *salt and pepper*
> *½ teaspoon thyme*
> *½ cup parsley, chopped*

Cook the rice about 20 minutes in the chicken broth. It should be tender, fluffy and well separated. Sauté the onion and celery in the butter; when the onion is transparent, add the currants and rosé and cook until the currants are plump. Then add everything else and mix well with the cooked rice. Chill the mixture, covered. After stuffing the birds turn the rest of the rice onto a double thickness of foil. Dot with more butter and seal the ends. This extra stuffing can be slipped in the oven for half an hour to heat. The foil package takes advantage of the hot oven and doesn't clutter up the stove top as heating in a double boiler would.

Souffléd Squash is not really a soufflé, but is delightfully delicate.

2 packages frozen cooked squash (12 ounces each)
¼ cup fine bread crumbs
salt, pepper and large dash nutmeg
3 eggs, separated

In the top of a double boiler thaw the frozen squash. Remove from heat and add the bread crumbs and seasonings. Next beat in the egg yolks and then the stiffly beaten egg whites. Pour the mixture into a baking dish (1½ to 2 quarts) which has been buttered and dusted with powdered sugar. Bake for about 30 minutes at 350 degrees.

String Beans Use frozen beans, cooked until just tender; drain and mix with sautéed almond slivers. Allow about 2 tablespoons of almonds per package of beans and enough butter to brown them nicely.

Chocolate-Chestnut Mold is wonderfully easy, particularly if you have been foresighted and prepared the chestnuts long ago.

CHESTNUTS With a sharp knife, gash each flat side twice in a cross. Cover chestnuts with boiling water and boil 20 to 30 minutes. Remove the shell and brown skin while chestnuts are still warm. Break nutmeats into small pieces and put in a blender with just enough water to maintain the vortex. Blend on high speed until smoothly puréed. Do about a cupful of chestnuts at a time and use as little water as possible. (The purée may be frozen; or freeze the whole nuts, dry-packed, after shelling and skinning.) For 8 servings of the mold you will need 1½ cups of purée.

>8 lady fingers
>2 ounces bitter chocolate
>3 tablespoons butter
>2 teaspoons water
>¾ cup granulated sugar
>2 tablespoons brandy
>1½ cups chestnut purée

First butter a small loaf pan, 7½ x 2¾ x 2 inches. Trim the lady fingers to 2-inch lengths; split them and line the long sides of the pan.

In the top of a double boiler, melt the chocolate and butter with the water. Add the chestnuts, sugar and brandy. Mix everything together, spoon into the prepared pan and chill at least 3 hours. Turn out on a serving dish and pile whipped cream generously on top. Slice between the lady fingers. The serving may seem small, but one slice of this rich dessert is really very adequate.

I know one family who have a happy tradition of selecting a mammoth rib roast of beef a couple of days after Thanksgiving. The butcher hangs it until December 23 or 24, when it is borne home to be admired for a while before it is roasted for Christmas.

This menu, with roast beef as its mainstay, has been very successful.

Bacon-Wrapped Oysters and Olives (page 42)
Blue Cheese Pastry (page 44)
Roast Beef

Horseradish Sauce (page 42)
Yorkshire Pudding
Mushroom-topped Tomatoes
Broccoli   Hollandaise Sauce
Plum Pudding
Fluffy Hard Sauce
Burgundy (served with the beef)
Brandy (served with coffee)

Roast Beef Choose a really big piece of meat, four ribs or more. There will be about 3 to 4 servings per pound. I usually count on 3 servings, allow 2 servings per person and then double the amount, for cold roast beef is a lovely thing to have on hand.

Have the butcher remove the chine and tie it back on to protect the eye of the roast in cooking. Trim any excess fat and rub meat all over with salt and pepper. Place, fat side up, in a shallow open roasting pan; sear in a 500-degree oven for 20 minutes. Reduce the heat to 325 degrees and cook 18 minutes per pound for rare and 20 to 22 minutes per pound for medium. Count the searing time in the total allowance. Remove the roast to a serving platter and let it stand in a warm place for 10 to 15 minutes before serving. Make gravy in the same way as for grouse (page 70), using beef stock or bouillon and omitting the currant jelly.

Yorkshire Pudding To bake the pudding in the same oven, you will have to increase the oven heat for a short time toward the end of the beef cooking period, so be sure to keep a watchful eye on the roast to prevent overcooking. Prepare the batter an hour or two before the dinner hour and chill, covered, in the refrigerator. The reason for the large quantity is that the pudding is intended to take the place of potatoes.

For 12 to 16 good-sized wedges:

2 cups flour
1 teaspoon salt
2 cups milk
4 eggs

Sift the flour and salt together in a mixing bowl. Stir in the milk and beat with a rotary or electric beater. Add the eggs, one at a time, beating strenuously after each addition. The eggs and milk should be at room temperature, and the batter should be of heavy-cream consistency. Place the batter, covered, in the refrigerator until ready to bake.

About ½ hour before serving time, take two 8-inch pie tins and spoon ¼ cup of fat drippings from the roast into each one. Put them in the oven to heat. Beat the chilled batter until large bubbles appear and divide it equally between the hot pie tins. Increase the heat of the oven to 450 degrees and bake until the pudding rises (about 15 minutes). Reduce the heat to 350 degrees and cook another 10 to 15 minutes until it is brown and crisp. Cut in wedges and serve on a hot platter or around the roast.

Mushroom-Topped Baked Tomatoes Choose small ones and allow 2 per person. Cut off the stem end, making a small deep hole. Push a teaspoonful each of butter and brown sugar into each one. Add salt and pepper and fine bread crumbs and dot with more butter. Bake at 350 degrees for about 15 minutes in a shallow pan with a little water in the bottom of it. Before serving, top each tomato with a large sautéed mushroom cap.

Hollandaise Sauce is no problem if a couple of helpful hints are followed. Use no metal utensils. Make the sauce in an earthenware or heatproof glass bowl over, *not in*, hot water. Don't let the water boil, and stir the mixture with a wooden spoon. For a cup of sauce:

> ¼ *pound butter*
> *4 egg yolks*
> *white pepper*
> *salt*
> *1 to 2 tablespoons lemon juice*

Divide the butter into 3 parts. Put the egg yolks and one part of the butter into the sauce bowl over hot water. Mix and stir constantly until the butter is melted. Then add the second piece of butter, stirring until it is melted. And then the third piece, continuing to stir. Remove the bowl from the heat and stir a couple of minutes longer. Add the pepper, salt and lemon juice. Replace the bowl over the hot water and stir some more until it thickens sufficiently. If the sauce should separate, beat in 1 to 2 tablespoons of boiling water to rebind it.

If more than a cup of sauce is required, a good way to stretch the basic ingredients is to mix in thoroughly an equal quantity of stiffly whipped cream and a little more lemon juice. Add these after the sauce is thickened. It then, technically, becomes **Sauce Mousseline,** but "What's in a name?"

Since hollandaise does not have to be served steaming, it can be made in advance. Just be sure that the food it will grace is served very hot.

Steam the Plum Pudding (page 9) for an hour or more before serving. Turn it out on a hot platter, douse it well with warmed brandy, light and serve.

Fluffy Hard Sauce is good with Plum Pudding and uses some of the egg whites left over from the hollandaise.

> *¼ cup butter, softened*
> *1½ cups powdered sugar, sifted*
> *2 tablespoons cream*
> *3 egg whites, stiffly beaten*
> *brandy*

Gradually cream the sugar into the butter; then add the cream and egg whites. Flavor with a tablespoon or more of brandy. Beat vigorously, pile in big heaps on serving dish and chill thoroughly.

No collection of Christmas recipes would be complete without Roast Goose.

You might have Hot Curry Dip (page 41) first, with iced shrimp and broccoli stems for dipping; and Cheddar-Chutney Puffs (page 40).

> *Roast Goose*
> *Apple-Onion Dressing*
> *Crab Apple Garnish*
> *Apple Sauce*
> *Orange-glazed Sweet Potatoes*
> *Creamed Spinach*
> *Water Cress and Romaine Salad*
> *Hot Mince Flambé*

Apple-Onion Dressing This recipe makes about 6 cups of dressing, which should be enough for a 10-pound goose. If you are doubtful or want more anyway, increase all the ingredients, using the same proportions.

> *fat from goose*
> *1 cup onion, coarsely chopped*
> *½ cup celery slivers*

¼ *cup water*
4 *cups soft bread crumbs, made from raisin bread**
2 *cups apple cubes, peeled*
1 *teaspoon salt*
1 *teaspoon poultry seasoning*
black pepper
**Or use plain bread for the crumbs and add*
    ¼ *cup raisins.*

Remove some of the fat from the uncooked goose and fry in a heavy iron skillet. When about ½ cup of fat has been rendered, remove the cracklings; add the onions and celery slivers and sauté 3 or 4 minutes. Remove from the heat and add the water.

In a large mixing bowl, mix the bread crumbs and apple cubes. Add the contents of the skillet and the seasonings and toss all together lightly.

Roast Goose   Stuff the goose with Apple-Onion Dressing and lace the openings securely. Place, breast side down, in a large open roasting pan with an inch of water in the bottom of the pan. Cook for about an hour in a 400-degree oven. Pour off all the liquid in the pan and discard it. Put a rack in the pan and place the goose on it, this time breast side up. Prick the skin all over with a sharp two-tined fork and return the bird to the oven. Reduce the heat to 325 degrees and roast for another 2½ hours, or until the skin is brown and crisp and the goose tender. Repeat the pricking of the skin with the fork 2 or 3 times during this period.

Orange-Glazed Sweet Potatoes can be prepared the day before and will be all ready to go into the oven. Boil sweet potatoes in their skins until *almost* tender. Peel them and cut in thick lengthwise slices, allowing 2 slices per person. Arrange them in a shallow, buttered casserole in overlapping rows. Store in refrigerator until ready for baking. Then sprinkle with salt and cover *thickly* with orange marmalade. Dot with butter and bake at 325 degrees for 30 to 40 minutes or until the potatoes are candied and brown.

Creamed Spinach Being a mad devotee of spinach in all forms, I tend to be overenthusiastic when planning quantity allowance. However, frozen spinach, when cooked, reduces itself to the point of providing only about 3 medium-sized servings per package. For 6 people, use 3 packages of frozen chopped spinach. Cook spinach only long enough to thaw and heat thoroughly; drain it *well*. Press out every bit of moisture you can possibly wring from it. Then make 2 cups of

RICH CREAM SAUCE

4 tablespoons butter
6 tablespoons flour
1 ½ cups milk
½ cup light sweet cream
salt, pepper and nutmeg
2 to 3 tablespoons sour cream

In the top of a double boiler over direct heat, melt the butter, blend in the flour and then gradually add the milk and cream. Stir this until it thickens, and season with salt, pepper and a generous dousing of nutmeg. Place pan with the sauce over hot water and mix in the cooked spinach. Cover and keep warm; just before serving, blend in the sour cream.

The salad is simplicity itself, but is really needed as a leavening between the rich main courses and the equally rich dessert.

Hot Mince Flambé is extremely festive, but is also very simple. Well in advance, make and bake pie crust cut in Christmas-tree shapes about 3 inches high. Decorate them, if you like, with dragées and colored sugars. Heat these in the oven for 5 or 10 minutes before they are to be served.

Meanwhile heat the mincemeat (page 10) in a double boiler, using about a cupful per person. Have a hot platter ready; mound the mincemeat in the center and stand the hot pastry trees around it, sticking one lower branch of each tree into the mincemeat to hold it erect. Douse with warmed brandy and serve flaming.

A fitting climax to this chapter would be the presentation of a whole suckling pig wearing a cranberry necklace to match his eyes. But it would be mere fantasy, for I have never found one available at the proper time. So let's settle for Cranberry-glazed Fresh Ham, and delicious it is too!

Sherry would be good served first, a choice of dry or cream, and with it a generous plate of Sesame Cheese Straws.

Chestnut Soup
Cranberry-Glazed Fresh Ham
Cranberry Sauce
Scalloped Grated Potatoes
Cauliflower with Peas
Tipsy Parson

Serve the soup in the living room for easier management of the main course. Replenish the cheese straws, for they go equally well with the soup.

Sesame Cheese Straws are cream-cheese pastry (page 44) cut in thin strips and sprinkled with sesame seeds before they are baked.

Chestnut Soup, in this version, is thin enough to be drinkable, so spoons aren't necessary for living-room service. The following ingredients make a little more than a quart:

1 bay leaf
2 whole cloves
1 thick slice of onion
2 or 3 celery tops
¼ teaspoon thyme
3 cups rich chicken broth
1½ cups chestnut purée (page 72)
1 cup light cream
salt and pepper to taste
½ cup sherry

Wrap the first 5 ingredients in a cheesecloth bag and boil them in the chicken broth for 10 to 15 minutes. Remove the cloth bag. Put the chestnut purée in the top of a double boiler and gradually add the hot chicken broth, blending smoothly. Place on direct heat, bring to a boil and then put the pan over hot water. Add the cream, salt, pepper and sherry. Keep soup hot in the double boiler until ready to serve.

Cranberry-Glazed Fresh Ham A 9- or 10-pound ham should serve 6 to 8 people and provide some leftovers or, with careful carving, up to 12 people with no leftovers.

Remove the ham skin and trim any excess fat. Rub ham all over with salt and pepper and let it stand at room temperature for an hour or two. Place it in an open roasting pan in a 400-degree oven for 30 minutes; then reduce the heat to 325 degrees. Roast for 25 minutes per pound, or until well done—about 4 hours for a 10-pound ham. Baste every 20 minutes with canned cranberry juice and pan drippings.

About ½ hour before the end of the total cooking time, remove the ham from the oven. Gash the fat in diamonds and spike it with cloves. Spread with 1 cup of Jellied Cranberry Sauce (page 106), which will melt on contact with the hot fat. Now baste the ham more frequently, every 10 minutes or so, to glaze it well. Garnish the serving platter with greenery and with whole raw cranberries, and serve a separate mold of the cranberry sauce.

Scalloped Grated Potatoes   No gravy is served with the ham, since the accompanying potatoes provide enough moistness.

For 6 people use 3 12-ounce packages of frozen grated potatoes containing 4 cakes each.

> *1 cup onion, finely chopped*
> *3 tablespoons flour*
> *5 tablespoons butter*
> *salt and pepper*
> *2 cups Half and Half, heated*

Butter a shallow casserole of a size to take half the potato cakes lying flat or only slightly overlapped. Put half the frozen patties in it, and the onion on top of them. Sprinkle the flour over them, dot with half the butter; salt and pepper them well and add the second layer of potato patties. The rest of the butter goes on this layer, and more seasonings. Pour the warm Half and Half over everything and cover the casserole with a sheet of foil. Bake at 325 degrees for an hour or a little longer, removing the foil after the first half-hour.

Cauliflower with Peas   Core a head of cauliflower, but leave it whole. If it has a few tender leaves attached at the base, leave them on. Steam it until it is *just* tender. Remove to a round serving platter and divide it into 6 or 8 wedges, but don't cut all the way through. Separate the wedges slightly and fill the crevices with cooked peas. Lemon juice and butter in liberal quantities are good on this.

Tipsy Parson (page 122) is a delicious finale. And plenty of good strong coffee.

CHAPTER NINE

Brunches and Lunches

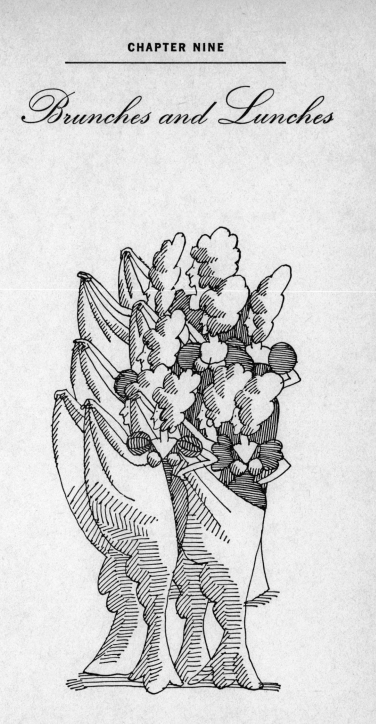

On the ninth day of Christmas my true love sent to me
Nine ladies dancing.

Food for brunch or lunch can be of the greatest variety. A brunch can be a real breakfast, a buffet, or a formal meal; and lunch allows the most unlimited exercise of imagination.

For brunches I highly recommend setting up the coffee service with the bar. Many people like a little straight brandy or rum in coffee either before or after eating. Confining all the liquids to one area simplifies the service. The choice of drinks is flexible. Bloody Marys (page 31), plain highballs, cocktails, champagne if the occasion warrants, are all appropriate. The spiced tomato juice that goes into a Bloody Mary may be served plain, and a choice of other fruit juices or clam juice. A pitcher of milk is often appreciated either for making a milk punch or to soothe a jumpy stomach.

For a "real breakfast" type of brunch the following menu has worked out well:

Cheese-Scrambled Eggs
Chopped Chives   Grated Parmesan Cheese
Kidney, Bacon and Mushroom Brochettes
Codfish Balls
Croissants with Marmalade
Baked Bananas

Cheese-Scrambled Eggs For 8 servings:

> ½ *cup light cream*
> 2 *3-ounce packages cream cheese*
> 12 *eggs, slightly beaten*
> *salt and pepper to taste*

Mash the cream cheese with the cream in the top of a double boiler and heat over hot water. Add the eggs, salt and pepper and cook very slowly, stirring now and then. These will hold over warm water for

87

20 minutes or so before serving. Sprinkle with chopped chives and/or grated parmesan cheese.

Kidney, Bacon and Mushroom Brochettes For 8 people use 16 to 24 skewers.

1 pound kidneys—veal, beef or lamb
½ pound bacon, cut in squares
2 canned button mushroom caps per skewer

Skin the kidneys, cut out the tubes and cut the kidneys in squares about the size of the mushroom caps. String the pieces of kidney and bacon alternately on skewers beginning and ending with a mushroom cap. Lay the skewers on a rack in a shallow baking pan. Squeeze a little lemon juice over them, and put a couple of pieces of bacon on top. Bake at 350 degrees for 25 to 30 minutes, turning them once. Or cook them in a frying pan in a little butter or bacon drippings.

Codfish Balls are easy to do in the oven. (I use a canned codfish-cake mixture and add a beaten egg, a tablespoon of cream and a lot of black pepper per 8-ounce can of codfish cakes.) Mix ingredients very well and form into *small* balls or cakes; roll them in flour. Melt and heat some butter in a shallow baking tin and roll the balls around in it. Bake at 350 degrees for 25 or 30 minutes.

Heat the croissants (page 103). They don't really demand butter with the marmalade filling; but there are some people who put butter on everything, so use your own judgment.

Baked Bananas are served in a chafing dish to keep them warm, but are cooked in the oven. Use 8 to 12 bananas, yellow but not quite ripe, peeled and cut in half lengthwise or in thick diagonal slices. Make a syrup of:

> *1 cup water*
> *1 cup brown sugar, light or dark*
> *½ cup white wine*
> *½ teaspoon cinnamon*
> *½ teaspoon nutmeg*
> *dash of powdered cloves*
> *1 tablespoon grated orange peel*

Mix all ingredients for syrup together, bring to a boil and simmer slowly. Brown the bananas in hot butter in a frying pan and transfer them to a buttered baking dish. Sprinkle with lemon juice and salt. Pour the hot syrup over them and cover with a ¼-inch layer of cornflake crumbs. Drizzle over the top the melted butter in which the bananas were browned. Bake at 350 degrees for 15 to 20 minutes. If you feel really festive, flame the bananas with ¼ cup dark rum just before serving.

The next menu was used for a Sunday brunch following a particularly hard Saturday which ended in the small hours of Sunday morning. It's a good choice for a New Year's Day of televiewing the bowl games too. Except for the coffee, *all* of it can be prepared the previous afternoon.

Chicken Tetrazzini
Salad of Raw Spinach Leaves and Celery Tops
Mild Garlic Dressing
Cherry Tomatoes Stuffed with Guacamole
Celery Curls   Olives
Fruitcake
Pineapple Sticks   Peeled Melon Slices

Assemble the Tetrazzini (page 116) in a casserole that will go from refrigerator to oven without inviting disaster—an enameled iron one, for instance.

Wash and dry the salad greens and put them in a plastic bag in the refrigerator. Make the salad dressing, and this part of the menu is ready for instant assembly in the morning.

The cherry tomatoes are simple to do and look so gay. Slice the tops off as many tomatoes as you need, and scoop out most of the pulp and seeds. A vegetable ball cutter is useful for this. Turn tomatoes upside down on a plate to drain while you make the Guacamole.

Guacamole is accomplished by mashing ripe avocados to a smooth purée. Season it with chili powder —½ teaspoon to a cup of avocado purée. Add salt and lemon juice to taste and a small amount of the scooped-out tomato pulp—about 2 tablespoons per cup of avocado.

Stuff the tomatoes. Cover them and refrigerate.

Cut the celery and place it in a bowl of water in the refrigerator. Prepare the melon slices and pineapple in sizes suitable for eating with fingers, and chill.

Cut a loaf of Italian bread in diagonal slices and butter the slices. Wrap the loaf in foil and store it in the refrigerator.

There is now no more to do until morning, when it is all a relatively simple matter of heating the Tetrazzini and bread, making coffee and serving the cold foods.

For a more formal "sit-down" luncheon, this menu is very good:

Canapé Parmigiana
Jellied Curry Ring
Chilled Green Beans Marinaded
in Olive Oil and Lemon Juice
Brioches   Butter
Cranberry Crumb Cake

Canapé Parmigiana For 6 canapés you will need 6 slices of toast with the crusts trimmed and 12 thin slices of eggplant cut the same size and shape as the bread.

> *1 8-ounce can tomato sauce*
> *3 tablespoons tomato paste*
> *1 clove garlic, minced*
> *1 cup fine bread crumbs*
> *½ cup grated Parmesan cheese*
> *chopped parsley (about ½ cup)*
> *olive oil*
> *6 thin slices Mozzarella cheese*

In a small saucepan, mix the tomato sauce, tomato paste and garlic and let simmer very slowly while you fry the eggplant. Cook the slices in hot olive oil for 3 or 4 minutes on each side, until they are soft and lightly browned. Drain on paper towels.

Coat the trimmed edges of the toast with olive oil by dipping them quickly in the oil in which the eggplant was fried. Then dip the edges in the chopped parsley, coating them well, and place the toast on a cookie sheet. Remove the tomato sauce from the heat. Mix together, in a small bowl, the bread crumbs and Parmesan cheese, and you are ready to build the canapés.

Spoon about a tablespoon of sauce onto each slice of toast. Use more sauce if the toast will absorb it without running over. Cover with a slice of eggplant, then sauce again and the mixed crumbs and cheese; next, the remaining slice of eggplant, topped with the Mozzarella. Do this much about an hour before you plan to serve them; then heat the canapés for 10 to 15 minutes in a 375-degree oven and serve sprinkled with the rest of the chopped parsley.

Shrimp is a good choice for the Jellied Curry Ring (page 104). Unmold it on shredded head lettuce; fill the middle with celery, radish, raisin and almond mixture (page 105) and serve with curry mayonnaise.

Cook the fresh or frozen beans the day before. Small whole green beans are the most attractive, but if they are not available, use the flat Italian variety. Make a marinade of 1 cup olive oil, ¼ cup lemon juice and salt and pepper. Coat the beans well with this and refrigerate, covered, until time to serve (when the marinade should be poured off).

Serve the Brioches (page 103) very hot, and when these have been removed from the oven, place the previously prepared Cranberry Crumb Cake (page 120) in the oven with the heat off to warm it slightly.

Soup is a fairly interesting way to handle an "Open House" that goes on all day with a large turnover of drop-ins. A choice of three—two of them hot and one cold—should be enough variety. Electric tureens are a big help toward effortless service, but any warming device that really works will do. Garnishes appropriate to the soups, such as lemon slices (for black bean), profiteroles, etc., are attractive additions to the buffet. Serve several kinds of small breads which do not require butter: cheese straws, perhaps, or small Italian bread sticks standing upright in a large goblet, and a choice of crackers.

Profiteroles are gay little puffs sometimes used instead of croutons. Make puffs (page 43) but use a pastry bag or salt spoons to form balls the size of large peas. They may be served plain or filled with pâté.

A good selection of soups for Christmas Eve includes: Green Turtle Soup with Sherry, and Purée Mongole, for the hot ones; and a well-chilled Strained Borsch.

Use one of the excellent canned turtle soups and lace it with sherry after heating. Provide more sherry to be added to individual servings and a bowl of chopped hard-cooked eggs for topping.

Purée Mongole may also be assembled from cans, but the following version, which will make about a quart, is a little better:

> 2 cups chicken broth
> 1 10-ounce package frozen peas
> ½ cup onion, chopped
> ¼ cup carrot, chopped
> ¼ teaspoon dried mint or sprig fresh mint
> 2 teaspoons curry powder
> 2 tablespoons butter
> 1 10½-ounce can condensed tomato soup
> equivalent volume of light cream
> salt and pepper to taste

Cook the peas, onion, carrot and mint in the chicken broth until very soft. Purée the vegetables in a blender or put them through a strainer. In the top of a double boiler over direct heat melt the butter and cook the curry powder in it for 2 or 3 minutes. Place the pan over hot water and add the puréed vegetables, the chicken broth in which they were cooked, the tomato and the cream. Taste and season with salt and pepper. Sometimes a little sugar is needed also.

Chopped chives and croutons are served with this,

and a sprinkling of chopped peanuts is surprisingly good too.

Strained Borsch, served very cold and garnished with sour cream, is a beautiful, ruby refreshment. This meatless version, which makes about 1 quart, is easily put together:

1 number 2½ can beets, chopped, undrained
½ cup onion, chopped
¼ cup carrot, chopped
2½ cups tomato juice
1 clove garlic
½ teaspoon dill seed
lemon juice, salt, sugar and pepper to taste

Simmer everything together for 15 to 20 minutes, strain and chill.

New Year's Day is a time for "restorative" soups, and a choice of these might include: Onion Soup, Black Bean with Sherry, and a cold Clam and Chicken Consommé.

Onion Soup can be laced with red wine, sherry or brandy. For a quart of the basic soup use:

2 cups onions, thinly sliced
4 tablespoons butter
1 tablespoon flour
4 cups beef bouillon
salt and pepper to taste

Cook the onions in the butter over very low heat, stirring frequently. When they are golden brown, sprinkle the flour over them and blend it well. Then add the bouillon and seasonings and bring the mixture to a boil, stirring constantly. Reduce the heat and simmer, covered, for about 20 minutes. For buffet service, provide thin rounds of toasted french bread and grated Parmesan or Gruyère cheese.

Black Bean Soup, when made at home, is a tedious, messy process. There are so many good canned black bean soups that it seems to me a waste of time to soak, simmer, purée, etc., all the ingredients called for. A little butter added to the hot soup improves the texture. Lace the soup well with sherry, and serve with it thinly sliced lemon, hard-cooked eggs and a bowl of finely diced ham.

Clam and Chicken Consommé is put together with canned soups, using equal quantities of chicken consommé and strong clam broth. Mix them together and heat for a few minutes to blend the flavors. Chill mixture well and serve either plain or with whipped cream.

The following two soups are included as dividends only because they are my absolute favorites, for two reasons—ease of preparation and delicious flavors.

Crab Soup

1 10½-ounce can condensed celery soup
equal quantity tomato juice
½ cup light cream
1 cup cooked crab meat, flaked
¼ cup dry white wine

Heat the celery soup and tomato juice in the top of a double boiler over direct heat and bring just to the boiling point. Place the pan over hot water; add the cream, blending it in well, and last of all put in the crab meat and white wine Turn off the heat and let the soup stand over the hot water just long enough to heat the crab meat.

Lemon Soup This is not the classic Greek version but a refreshing cold soup. It is made by grating the zest of a medium-sized lemon into a pint of chicken consommé. Simmer for 5 or 6 minutes and add lemon juice to taste. The soup should be quite sour and lemony. Strain out the lemon peel and chill the soup well before serving.

CHAPTER TEN

Five Gold Rings

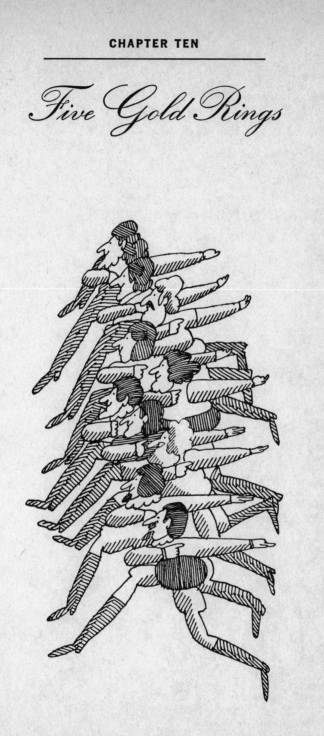

On the tenth day of Christmas my true love sent to me
Ten lords a-leaping.

Here you will find more than the Five Gold Rings celebrated in song. They run the gamut of golds from white through yellow, green, rose and red, and there is one for almost any occasion.

Ice Rings frozen with fruits—lemon slices, mint, etc.—are a decorative way of chilling punches. They are especially good for a smallish bowl, for the punch can be ladled through the center of the ring.

Draw as much tap water in a bowl as you will need to fill the ring. Stir it up every 3 or 4 minutes to release the air bubbles. Air bubbles make the ice cloudy. Keep doing this for about 15 minutes. Partially freeze a layer of this water in the ring, making it deep enough to hold the decorations securely, or about ⅓ the depth of the ring. Chill the remaining water. When the ice in the ring is of a slushy sherbet consistency, arrange on it a wreath of prepared décor: thin lemon slices slashed from the center to the edge and twisted to stand upright; seedless green grapes in small clusters; "holly" of red maraschino cherries with leaves cut from green cherries or thin cucumber peel; whole fresh berries; preserved or fresh kumquats; mint; lemon thyme and rose geranium leaves are a few suggestions. When the ring with the fruit added is again frozen solid, pour the rest of the chilled water over it and complete the freezing.

In adding the fruit be sure that the flavors will enhance the type of punch you're making if, while you're serving it, the ring should melt enough to release the decorations. Having the punch thoroughly chilled before adding the unmolded ring minimizes this possibility.

Pâtés and spreads are attractive served in rings. Both the Baked Liver Pâté (page 37) and Jellied Pâté (page 38) can be prepared in ring molds, and any cocktail spread that is stiff enough to pack tightly, such as a blending of cheeses, can be made in a mold.

Roquefort Ring is intended to be thinly sliced and served with Melba toast. It makes a good salad too, unmolded on greenery, its middle filled with white grapes and avocado balls.

> *1 tablespoon gelatin*
> *¼ cup cold water*
> *2 cups creamed cottage cheese*
> *2 3-ounce packages cream cheese*
> *½ cup crumbled Roquefort cheese*
> *½ cup light cream*
> *½ cup chopped ripe olives*
> *1 teaspoon salt*
> *3 or 4 dashes hot pepper sauce*

Soak the gelatin in the cold water and dissolve it over hot water. Mash the cheeses, cream and seasonings together and beat until very smooth. Add the gelatin and ripe olives, mixing all the ingredients together. Pack the mixture in an oiled 1-quart ring mold and chill until it is firm.

Swedish Tea Rings are beautiful to behold and need not be confined to tea-time. The following ingredients will make one 9-inch ring, but the recipe can be doubled easily:

> *1 egg*
> *¼ cup warm water*
> *½ cake compressed yeast*

2 cups all-purpose flour, sifted
½ teaspoon salt
1 tablespoon sugar
¾ teaspoon powdered cardamon
1 cup butter

Beat the egg well, add the warm water and dissolve the yeast in this liquid. Place in the refrigerator for about 15 minutes while you blend, in a large bowl the flour, salt, sugar, cardamon and ¼ cup of the butter. Make a hole in the middle of this mixture and pour the chilled liquid into it. Work all together and knead about 2 minutes or until smooth. Form into a ball, wrap loosely in wax paper and chill 20 to 30 minutes. Cream the remaining butter to a very soft consistency. Roll the dough into an oblong a scant ½ inch thick. Cover ⅔ of the dough with small dabs of butter, using ⅓ of the total amount of butter remaining. Fold ⅓ of unbuttered dough over on ⅓ of the buttered portion and then fold again to form 3 layers with the unbuttered layer in the middle. Give the dough a quarter turn on the board. Roll out again, repeating the same performance of dabs of butter, folding and turning, using another ⅓ of the butter. Finally, do it once more. Wrap in wax paper and chill 2 or 3 hours.

Roll again, on a lightly floured board, into a sheet about 11 x 28 to 11 x 30 inches. Spread about a cupful of filling (see below) evenly over the dough and roll up like a jelly roll from the narrow end. Place on a buttered baking sheet, dampen the ends so that they will stick together and join them, forming a ring. Now take floured scissors and make bias gashes about an inch apart through the outside of the ring to within an inch or so of the center. Separate these slices slightly so that the filling is partially exposed. Cover the pre pared ring with a damp cloth and allow to rise until almost double in bulk. Bake at 400 degrees for about 25 minutes.

Fillings for tea rings can be as simple as plain jam or marmalade; or melted butter spread on first and then an even sprinkling of chopped nuts, raisins or currants, spices and sugar. A little grated lemon peel adds zest to nearly all fillings. Blended mixtures should be cooled slightly before they are spread on the dough. The following recipes will fill one 9-inch ring:

DATE FILLING

> ¼ *cup butter*
> ⅓ *cup light brown sugar*
> ¾ *cup dates, finely chopped*
> ¼ *cup almonds, finely chopped*
> ½ *teaspoon grated lemon peel*
> *dash of nutmeg and a little salt*

Melt the butter. Add the brown sugar and cook over very low heat for 2 or 3 minutes, stirring constantly. Remove from heat and add everything else.

APPLE-RAISIN FILLING

> ¼ *cup butter*
> ¼ *cup light brown sugar*
> *1 cup apples, peeled, chopped*
> ½ *cup raisins*
> *1 teaspoon cinnamon*
> ½ *teaspoon lemon peel, grated*
> ¼ *teaspoon salt*

Mix everything together in a small saucepan and simmer 3 or 4 minutes.

NUT FILLING

> ½ *cup nuts, ground (pecans, walnuts, etc.)*
> ½ *cup sugar*
> ½ *teaspoon vanilla or almond extract*

3 tablespoons candied orange peel, chopped
1 egg
milk

Combine everything except the egg and milk. Then beat in the egg and thin the mixture with milk until it has a good, gooey spreading consistency.

The basic dough for Tea Rings can be baked in other shapes too:

Croissants Cut the rolled dough in 3-inch squares and then diagonally in triangles. Roll up from the wide end and curve them in crescents. Place on a greased baking tin. Cover with a damp cloth and let rise until almost doubled in bulk. Bake at 375 degrees for 15 minutes.

These can also have a couple of teaspoons of filling rolled up in them, if you like; or use plain orange marmalade.

Brioche shapes are attractive. If you have fluted brioche tins, that's wonderful; but muffin pans will do as well. Omit the cardamon powder in making the dough. Grease the pans and form dough into balls of a size to half-fill them. Make a crisscross cut in the tops of each. Make smaller balls of dough, about ¼ the size of the first ones, and insert them in the cuts of the large balls. Cover with a damp cloth and let rise to almost double size. After they have risen, brush them lightly with beaten egg yolk. Don't plaster it on, for if it covers the joint between the two balls of dough it will interfere with further rising during baking. Bake about 15 minutes at 375 degrees. If the tops brown too quickly, cover them loosely with a sheet of foil or brown paper.

Cheese Roll Ring uses "bakery" butter-gem rolls—the kind that are baked in thin vertical layers. Partially separate the layers and insert thin bits of cheddar cheese between every two or three layers. Place the rolls in a pie tin, making a ring of them, and press them down with your hand so that they are flattened slightly. Put more cheese between the individual rolls so that they stick together in one large ring. Heat in a moderate oven until they are warm and the cheese is browned.

Jellied Curry Ring is a sort of simplified Chicken Indienne, but the meat need not be chicken necessarily. It is also delicious made with turkey, shrimp, crab or veal.

> *2 teaspoons curry powder*
> *½ teaspoon salt*
> *1 cup boiling water*
> *1 package celery-flavored gelatin*
> *1 cup cold water*
> *2 teaspoons vinegar or lemon juice*
> *1 cup cooked diced meat*
> *¼ cup diced green pepper*

Put the curry powder and salt in the boiling water and cook for a minute or two. Remove from the heat and add the gelatin, stirring to dissolve it thoroughly. Then add the cold water and vinegar. Chill until thickened but not set, and add the meat and green pepper. Spoon the mixture into an oiled mold and chill again for 2 to 3 hours.

Mayonnaise flavored with a little more curry powder, or thinned with a little juice from mango chutney, is a good dressing to serve with this.

Fill the center of the ring with something crisp in the nature of a Sambal (page 125). A combination of celery, radishes, almonds (all thinly sliced) and whole white raisins in equal quantities is good; or sliced celery and diced apples with a few nuts. Bind the fillings with a little mayonnaise.

Jellied Ring of Artichokes and Avocado makes a delightful combination of color and flavor.

> *1 9-ounce package frozen artichoke hearts*
> *1 cup boiling water (in which artichokes were cooked)*
> *1 package celery-flavored gelatin*
> *1 cup cold water*
> *1 tablespoon lemon juice*
> *½ teaspoon salt*
> *¼ teaspoon hot pepper sauce*
> *avocado slices, rolled in more lemon juice*

Cook the artichokes as directed on the package. Drain, reserving 1 cup of the water, and chill them.

Dissolve the gelatin in the boiling artichoke water; then add the cold water, lemon juice and seasonings. Pour a layer, ½ inch deep, into an oiled ring mold and chill until firm.

Arrange the artichoke hearts evenly around the ring mold and fill spaces between them with avocado slices, packing them in tightly to form a continuous circle of vegetables. Add more (but not all) of the gelatin, which has been chilled thick (but not firm), and return the mold to the refrigerator to set and anchor the vegetables firmly. Then add the rest of the cooled gelatin. Chill for at least 2 hours before serving.

A vegetable served in a circle, the center filled with a contrasting vegetable, not only looks beautiful but conserves serving space.

Chestnut Ring filled with buttered peas or tiny creamed onions is a happy addition to many menus.

1 ½ cups chestnut purée (page 72)
3 tablespoons flour
salt, pepper and nutmeg to taste
1 tablespoon onion, grated
¾ cup milk
4 egg whites

Combine, in a heavy saucepan, the chestnut purée, flour, seasonings and onion. Add the milk gradually and cook over low heat for about 5 minutes, stirring constantly. Remove from the heat and allow to cool while you beat the egg whites stiff. Fold in the egg whites, and pour into a buttered mold. Set the mold on a rack in a baking pan filled with hot water. Bake about 30 minutes at 325 degrees. To serve, run a knife around the mold to loosen the contents, and invert on a hot plate.

Jellied Cranberry Sauce is lovely in a ring mold, but, of course, can be molded in any shape. Chilled in a shallow pan, it can be cut with a cookie cutter into fancy shapes for garnishes.

For 1 quart of washed and drained cranberries, use 2 cups boiling water and 2 cups sugar. First boil the cranberries in the water for 20 minutes. Skim out the berries and put them through a strainer. Return the pulp, free of skins and seeds, to the water. Add the sugar and bring to a boil, stirring well. Pour into a wet mold and chill until firm.

Cranberry Mold is a dessert appropriate to the season:

> *1 tablespoon gelatin*
> *½ cup water*
> *2 1-pound cans cranberry sauce (either whole-berry or strained)*
> *½ cup chopped walnuts*
> *1 cup apples, peeled, diced*
> *1 tablespoon orange rind, grated*
> *½ cup Cointreau*

In the top of a double boiler, soak the gelatin in the water and dissolve it over hot water. Add the cranberry sauce and heat until the sauce is syrupy. Remove from the heat and add everything else. Pour into a 6-cup oiled ring mold. Chill for several hours until set, and serve with sour cream.

For a very good molded salad, omit the Cointreau, add ½ cup chopped celery and serve with mayonnaise.

Nesselrode Puffs are a sort of Croquembouche—not built up into a tree form, but just a two-tiered ring, which is much easier to put together though not quite as impressive.

To serve 6 to 8 people, bake 24 puffs (page 43) about 2 inches in diameter finished size. At the same time bake a 9-inch circle of pie-crust dough rolled ¼ inch thick.

Next make the filling. Instead of fresh whipping cream I use for this the dry, non-dairy type of whipped topping. If the puffs have to sit around for a while before they are served, there is less danger of spoilage. Mix 2 large-sized envelopes (the size that makes about 2 cups of topping per package) according to package directions. Add 1 jar (10 ounces) of prepared Nesselrode Sauce. Fill the puffs. If there is any filling left over, it can be kept in the refrigerator for several days.

Place 1 cup water and 1½ cups sugar in a large heavy pan. Stir constantly and cook over moderate heat until the syrup is caramelized and thick.

Put the baked pastry circle on its serving plate. Dip the filled puffs quickly, one at a time, into the hot caramel, and arrange them around the edge of the pastry ring. Make a second inner ring of the puffs, and then put the rest of them on top of the double ring. Dust with confectioners' sugar. To serve, pull the puffs apart, using two forks.

CHAPTER ELEVEN

Ordinary Days

On the eleventh day of Christmas my true love sent to me
Eleven pipers piping.

Rather than use precise menus for this chapter, I shall toss out a few thoughts on several versatile mainstays, useful for many occasions.

The first is a savory "Freezer Stew." Pack it in small containers: pints preferably, and no larger than quarts. It is easier to thaw smaller sizes and to estimate the correct number of servings from them: a pint for two people, two pints for three or four, etc. The stew is frozen without vegetables; these may be freshly cooked at the time of serving, they may be leftovers, or taken from cans, as circumstances indicate. Lamb or veal kidneys, and a few mushrooms, sliced, sautéed and added to the basic stew, make a wonderful pie filling.

Freezer Stew Have the butcher cut a large chuck roast into steaks 1 inch thick; remove the bones and any large chunks of fat, and keep adding steaks until 8 pounds of boneless weight is reached. Then ask him to weigh the bones and trimmings and charge you the cheaper "bone-in" price. Take the bones home and you have both stock material and animal treats.

> *8 pounds beef, cut in 1-inch squares*
> *¼ pound butter*
> *2 cloves garlic, peeled*
> *2 cups onion, coarsely chopped*
> *1 cup carrots, coarsely chopped*
> *½ cup celery tops*
> *1 cup dry red wine*
> *10 to 12 whole peppercorns*
> *3 bay leaves*
> *1 teaspoon allspice*
> *1 teaspoon basil*
> *6 cups bouillon, canned or made with cubes*

salt and Worcestershire sauce to taste
1 ½ cups raw potatoes, diced (for thickening)

Heat and salt heavily a large iron frying pan. Sear the meat thoroughly in this. (It is a boring task that seems to take hours, but the results are well worth it.) Transfer the meat to a big kettle or Dutch oven. Melt the butter in the frying pan and sauté the garlic, onion, carrots and celery tops. When they are golden brown, add the wine. Scrape and stir to loosen all the pan drippings, and add all of this to the meat. Then add everything else. Cover the pot and simmer very slowly about 3 hours, or until the meat is tender. Cool, pour off the gravy and purée it in a blender. Combine it with the meat and pack the stew in freezer containers. When reheating, add a little red wine if the gravy seems too thick.

Be sure to save any leftovers from this stew. I recently made a marvelous soup which defied analysis but was delicious. The ingredients were approximately 1 cup of leftover beef and kidney pie (including a small piece of crust) and a tin of tomato bouillon, all smashed together in the blender, heated and served with sour cream and chives. Remember this blender soup maneuver for *any* leftovers, even salad.

Blender Salad Soup is made by mixing a cup of chicken broth or consommé and 1 ½ teaspoons flour. Put this in a blender and add 2 cups of leftover green salad, *with* the dressing, and purée until smooth. If there is more salad, use more broth and flour proportionately. Cook the soup slowly for about an hour, stirring now and then. It should be thick. Garlic croutons and/or a dusting of Parmesan cheese are good with this.

Hash is another delight which is worth making from scratch even though the chopping and dicing seem interminable. Using a meat grinder is faster, but both the potatoes and meat gain immensely in eye appeal if they are uniformly diced. Don't let the potatoes get mushy when you boil them. They have more cooking time coming to them while the hash is browning and are easier to cut when they are fairly firm.

Also, don't overdo the proportions: a good one is 1½ cups meat to 1 cup potatoes (certainly no greater quantity of potato than meat).

Corned Beef Hash I usually use the canned Argentine beef for this. (I once heard that in the Argentine the whole animal is corned, choice cuts as well as brisket. It may be an unfounded rumor, but Argentine corned beef has seemed to taste better ever since.) Have the meat very cold for easy dicing. Put the meat and potatoes into a mixing bowl. Grated onion goes in next, in the proportion of 2 tablespoons per cup of the combined meat and potatoes; then lots of freshly ground black pepper. Taste and add salt if needed. Mix all the ingredients well with a little cream —not very much, just enough to bind them. Cover with foil or wax paper, and put the hash in the refrigerator to chill thoroughly before browning.

RED FLANNEL HASH adds diced cooked beets to the corned beef hash recipe. Allow 1 cup each of potatoes and beets to 1½ cups of meat.

Make other hashes in the same way, using leftover beef or lamb, ham, etc. If there is any gravy, use this instead of cream.

To cook the hash, melt and heat fat (butter or bacon drippings, etc.) to a depth of ⅛ inch. in a heavy skillet.

Press the chilled hash into the pan, spread out evenly about 1½ inches thick. Reduce the heat to very low and cook until a rich brown crust forms on the bottom. Serve folded in half like an omelet. Or bake the hash at 350 degrees in a buttered shallow casserole for about ½ hour. Or use individual casseroles. When the hash has baked about 20 minutes, make a depression in it with the bottom of a glass or custard cup, and carefully slip in an egg. Put a small piece of butter on top of the yolk and bake until the egg is set.

A thick slice of green pepper makes an attractive corral for an egg. Press the raw pepper slice into the hash, allowing it to project enough to contain the egg.

Grated Swiss cheese is good on ham hash. Sprinkle it on top after the hash is about two-thirds cooked, and let it melt and brown. This, of course, has to be done in an oven.

Chicken Hash usually is just another version of creamed chicken—not browned, but served with something starchy, such as corn bread or rice, or in pastry cases. Very good it is, but it somehow doesn't seem to be "hash." This recipe, however, is different and more hashlike. For 4 fairly generous servings:

> ½ cup fine bread crumbs
> ¾ cup condensed cream of chicken or cream
>   of mushroom soup
> 1 4-ounce can chopped mushrooms, drained
> 2 tablespoons parsley, chopped
> 2 tablespoons chives, chopped
> 2 cups cooked chicken, diced
> ½ teaspoon oregano
> salt and pepper to taste

Mix everything together, chill the mixture and, when ready to cook, melt the 3 tablespoons of butter in a heavy frying pan. Add the hash and cook slowly until crusted. Since this burns easily, an asbestos mat on the burner is a good idea. Serve in an omelet fold like corned beef hash.

Clam Hash can be made the same way, with drained minced clams used instead of chicken.

Tetrazzinis are controversial concoctions. What all the recipes agree on, however, is dividing of the sauce equally between the spaghetti or macaroni and the meat; making a hole in the dressed pasta and placing the meat in the hole. Then the whole thing is coated with grated cheese. Not everyone agrees on the type of cheese, but whether you use Parmesan, Romano, Swiss or plain Cheddar, it is still a Tetrazzini. As for the rest of the ingredients, anything goes, and that makes Tetrazzinis an elegant solution to the leftovers problem.

It is most commonly made with chicken or turkey, but other things blend amiably with the mushroom sauce and are equally good: veal, for instance, or sea foods. A delicious Lenten Tetrazzini uses a combination of cauliflower fleurettes, flat green Italian beans and thin carrot slices instead of meat. This also makes a good all-in-one vegetable offering to accompany plain broiled chicken or a roast. The following recipe is extravagant, calorie-loaded and *very* good. It will produce 6 to 8 servings.

Chicken Tetrazzini

½ pound thin spaghetti
1 pound fresh mushrooms
4 tablespoons butter (for sautéing mushrooms)
3 cups chicken, cut in fairly large strips
½ cup almonds, blanched, slivered
¼ cup parsley, chopped
3 tablespoons butter or chicken fat (for sauce)
2 tablespoons flour
2 cups chicken broth
salt and pepper to taste
1 cup heavy cream
¼ cup (or more) dry white wine
grated Parmesan cheese

Boil the spaghetti. While it is cooking, slice the mushrooms lengthwise, leaving the stems attached, and sauté them in the 4 tablespoons of butter. (You can use canned mushrooms, but they won't taste as good.)

In a bowl, combine the cooked drained spaghetti, the mushrooms and any butter that has not been absorbed. Place the chicken, almonds and parsley in another bowl.

Make a sauce by melting the 3 tablespoons of butter or chicken fat and cooking the flour in it for 2 or 3 minutes. Gradually add the broth and seasonings and cook slowly until the mixture is quite thick. Remove it from the heat and add the cream and wine.

Divide the sauce equally between the pasta and the meat. Butter a casserole big enough to hold everything. (It should be wider than it is deep to allow a maximum of cheese topping.) Place the contents of the spaghetti bowl in the casserole, and make a hole in the middle, pouring the contents of the chicken bowl into it. Now coat the entire top heavily with the cheese. Bake at 350 degrees until everything is heated thoroughly and the cheese is brown (about 30 to 40 minutes if the ingredients are cold, less if the ingredients are still warm).

For economy, you may use more flour and milk in the basic sauce, instead of the heavy cream and wine, or make it with condensed cream of mushroom soup. (It will not be as rich and tasty.) The almonds are not essential, nor is the parsley. You might substitute chopped chives for the parsley, or add some chives anyway. Sliced ripe olives and/or a few capers are good with sea food instead of the almonds.

Lasagne is another controversial pasta dish. Some recipes make little balls of the meat; some add Italian sausage or sliced kidney, and some omit meat altogether. And, as in Tetrazzinis, the cheese used can be almost any variety. The following recipe will fill a baking dish 18 x 8 x 2½ inches:

> *1 number 2½ can Italian peeled tomatoes*
> *2 8-ounce cans tomato sauce*
> *1 bay leaf*
> *1 teaspoon basil*
> *1 teaspoon oregano*
> *½ to ⅔ cup olive oil*
> *2 cloves garlic, minced*
> *1 cup onion, minced*
> *1 pound lean beef, ground*
> *¼ pound Italian sausage, thinly sliced*
> *2 teaspoons salt*
> *pepper to taste*
> *½ pound lasagne noodles*
> *¼ pound Mozzarella cheese, thinly sliced*
> *½ pound Ricotta cheese*
> *¼ pound grated Parmesan cheese*

Start simmering in a saucepan the tomatoes, tomato sauce, bay leaf, basil and oregano. Heat ⅓ cup of the olive oil in a frying pan and sauté the garlic and onion for 2 or 3 minutes. Then add the beef, breaking it up with a fork. Cook just until the meat loses its red color. Add the contents of the frying pan and the salt and pepper to the tomatoes and simmer very slowly, uncovered, for about 2 hours. The sauce may be made a day or two ahead of time and reheated when the casserole is assembled.

Fry the sausage in a little more olive oil. Boil the lasagne noodles according to package directions; drain and separate the noodles. If you add a tablespoon of oil to the cooking water, the noodles will be easier to handle.

Grease a shallow oblong baking dish with olive oil, and put about ½ cup of the prepared sauce into the dish. Over this sauce, place ⅓ of the noodles in a basket-weave pattern; then a layer of Mozzarella; then ⅓ of the remaining meat sauce and ½ the sausages; a layer of Ricotta; and then a generous dousing of Parmesan. Continue with noodles, Mozzarella, sauce the rest of the sausages, Ricotta and ½ of the remaining Parmesan. On the third and final layer of noodles, pour the rest of the sauce and finish with Parmesan cheese. Bake about 30 minutes at 375 degrees. Remove the dish from the oven, and let it stand for 10 to 15 minutes before cutting.

Ratatouille is a wild combination of vegetables which is doubly useful because it is equally delicious either hot or cold. Remnants of it make a marvelous blender soup or can be smashed up and added to any tomato-based sauce with lovely results. Cook it in a large flameproof, covered casserole. If you use a glass one, the vegetables show off to beautiful advantage. Slice everything very thin and place in the casserole in layers, in the sequence given in the ingredients list. For 6 to 8 generous servings:

½ *cup olive oil*
2 *cloves garlic*
1 *medium eggplant, peeled*
3 *large onions, peeled*
4 *green peppers, seeded*
5 *small zucchini, unpeeled*
6 *small tomatoes, peeled*
salt and pepper

Heat ⅓ cup of the olive oil in the casserole and add the garlic. Cook for 2 or 3 minutes, but don't let it brown. Then arrange the vegetables in the casserole, seasoning each layer as you progress. Sprinkle the rest of the olive oil on the surface. Cover the casserole and cook over very low heat for 35 to 40 minutes. Then remove the cover and cook 10 minutes longer to reduce the liquid. A little more olive oil and some lemon juice should be sprinkled on the top when this is served cold.

Here are a few miscellaneous desserts:

Coffee Chiffon Mixture, a lovely, light dessert, is one favorite. The following will fill a 9- or 10-inch pie crust:

2 *tablespoons gelatin*
½ *cup coffee liqueur (Kahlua, Tia Maria, etc.)*
3 *cups hot, strong coffee*
¾ *cup sugar*
½ *pint whipping cream*
½ *teaspoon salt*
1 *tablespoon vanilla extract*
shaved bitter chocolate

In a large mixing bowl, soften the gelatin in the liqueur. Add the sugar and hot coffee, and stir until the gelatin and sugar are dissolved. Chill, and when almost firm, beat with an electric or rotary beater until the mixture is light and fluffy and free of lumps. Whip the cream with the salt and vanilla extract and blend into the gelatin mixture. Now do whatever you like with it. Mound it in sherbet glasses; or place it in a previously baked pie shell—either pastry, crumb or coconut; or spoon it into a serving bowl. However you plan to serve it, garnish it with shaved bitter chocolate before chilling and refrigerate at least 2 hours.

Coconut Crust Thickly butter a 10-inch glass pie plate, and press in firmly 1 package (4 ounces) of shredded coconut, building up the edges as much as possible. Bake 10 to 12 minutes at 375 degrees. Keep an eye on it, for it burns easily.

Cranberry Crumb Cake is a delicious seasonal dessert. Serve it warm with vanilla ice cream or plain cream. For 6 to 8 servings:

1 tablespoon cornstarch
¼ cup water
4 cups fresh cranberries, washed and drained
1 cup sugar
½ teaspoon mace

Mix all the ingredients together in a heavy saucepan. Bring to a boil and simmer, stirring constantly, until the cranberries begin to burst. Remove from the fire and cool.

2 cups biscuit mix
2 tablespoons sugar
2 tablespoons butter
1 egg
¼ cup milk

Mix to a cornmeal consistency the biscuit mix, sugar and butter. Beat the egg in the milk and add it to the biscuit mixture Mix lightly with a fork until just combined. Put the dough in a buttered 9-inch round glass baking dish (deeper than a pie plate) and pour the cooled cranberry mixture over it. Make a topping of:

> ½ *cup biscuit mix*
> ¼ *cup sugar*
> *2 tablespoons butter*

Mix with a fork until it is crumbly and sprinkle evenly over the cranberries. Bake 25 to 30 minutes at 400 degrees.

Trifles are desserts "built" of cake slices—yellow, sponge, angel food, etc., fresh or stale. The cake is well sprinkled with something alcoholic, like brandy, sherry or rum; and sometimes spread with jam or jelly, particularly raspberry. Almond slivers are stuck into it, and a boiled custard is poured over it. A great heap of whipped cream goes on next, and the cream is sometimes garnished with more almonds, maraschino cherries or sprigs of mint. All this is done in a deep glass or silver bowl, and the whole thing is chilled for 3 hours or more before it is served.

Boiled Custard for Trifle Lightly beat 3 egg yolks in the top of a double boiler. Add 2 cups of scalded milk, ¼ cup of sugar and a little salt. Cook over, not in, hot water, and don't let the water boil. Stir constantly until the sauce coats the spoon. Add 1 teaspoon of vanilla extract; remove from the heat and allow the sauce to cool. This makes slightly more than 1 pint.

Tipsy Parson is a delicious type of trifle. You will need the following:

double recipe of Boiled Custard
1 round 10-inch angel cake
1 cup almonds, slivered
1 cup (more or less) sherry
1 pint whipping cream
1 tablespoon sugar
maraschino cherries, cut in half

Cut the cake horizontally in 3 slices. Place the bottom layer in a serving bowl. Stick half the almonds into it, and douse it well with sherry. Spoon some of the custard over it and cover with the middle cake layer. Repeat the process, using the rest of the almonds, more sherry and custard. Put on the top layer. No almonds this time, but more sherry and custard. Pour any extra custard into the hole. Now beat the cream stiff, flavoring it with the sugar and a little sherry. Mask the cake on top and sides with this, and garnish with the maraschino cherry halves. Chill thoroughly before serving.

I have made very little mention of New Year's Eve or New Year's Day. The menus appearing in other chapters are adaptable to most entertainments you might have in mind. Just be sure to eat whatever, in your locality, is thought to bring good luck for the coming year. In mine, it is black-eyed peas and hog jowl—an unattractive dish, nevertheless served every New Year's Day. Presumably, good fortune is assured. It's a comforting thought, and Happy New Year to you!

Chutney is essential—mango chutney if possible, but peach or apple chutney makes an acceptable substitute. Preserved fruits of all kinds—kumquats, chopped guava, mandariṇ orange sections, ginger root, etc.— and dried fruits such as currants, raisins or strips of dried apricots are suggestions for sweet condiments.

Sambal Sauce dresses any fresh chopped vegetable, or sea food such as lobster or shrimp.

COCONUT CREAM is used as a base. The ingredients are:

> *a fresh coconut*
> *garlic*
> *onion*
> *cayenne pepper or hot pepper sauce*

Grate the coconut meat into a saucepan. Pour on cold water to barely cover the nutmeat and bring to a boil. Remove the pan from the heat; allow coconut to steep 10 to 15 minutes and strain, pressing out all the liquid. To this liquid, or coconut milk, add garlic that has been put through a press, about one half of a small clove per cup of milk. Add grated onion, using 2 tablespoons per cup of milk, a generous pinch of cayenne or dash of hot pepper sauce. Bottle the mixture and allow it to "ripen" for a day or two in the refrigerator.

Using only enough to moisten the vegetables, try this sauce with well-drained and chopped fresh tomatoes; with cucumber, seeded, diced and crisped in cold water; shredded lettuce or nasturtium leaves; chopped sweet green pepper or green chilies; onions of any variety; celery; thinly sliced radishes oɪ diced tart apples. These, of course, may be served just as they are, or with only a little salt and lemon juice, but the sauce adds an interesting flavor

For Epiphany, Curry of Lamb is especially appropriate. Its sauce is full of spices of the East, suggesting the Three Wise Men. The following menu is excellent for buffet service and will produce a delicious salute to the Three Kings:

Curry of Lamb
Rice
Small Bowls of Sambals (Condiments)
Fried Onion Rings   Eggplant Slices
Puppadums
Pineapple Quarters
Beer

First of all, the term *curried* usually denotes a dish of almost any variety of food that has been previously cooked and then reheated in a sauce flavored with curry powder. Curried Eggs and Sausage (page 64) is an example. But *curry of* lamb (or chicken, etc.) means a real production. The meat is cooked in the sauce, and the procedure is much the same as making stew.

Beer is the perfect partner for all curries.

The accompanying condiments, called *Sambals*, are both numerous and elaborately exotic. One hears of 20- and 30- "boy" curries, meaning, in plainer words, a curry accompanied by 20 or 30 different condiments, with a serving "boy" to pass each one. For practical purposes, 10 or 12 Sambals can make an impressive display; and if a few of each category are selected, they provide enough choices for individual tastes. But the more the merrier, as long as they do something definite toward adding to flavor or texture. They should be crisp, or salty, or sweet, or sour, or *something*. The exception is hard-cooked eggs with the yolks and whites separately chopped. They do nothing at all for the curry but, for some reason, are traditional; and they count as two more "boys."

CHAPTER TWELVE

Curry for Twelfth Night

On the twelfth day of Christmas my true love sent to me
Twelve drummers drumming.

Grated mild cheese is good; and chopped nuts of all kinds, particularly peanuts.

Coconut, either freshly grated or canned, and tinned Chinese noodles add crispness.

Small sprigs of parsley or mint, sweet and sour pickles and pickle relish, chopped olive, ham, thin rounds of Vienna or other sausage, raw or pickled mushrooms are some more suggestions.

Chipped beef or salt mackerel, liberally doused with cayenne, dried out in a slow oven and crumbled, makes a good sambal, combining crispness, saltiness and pepperiness.

A tiny bowl of hot pepper seeds is another accompaniment. It's a good idea to identify it, though. One friend who serves this props in front of the bowl a card which states *HOT* in large red letters.

Bombay Duck, which may be bought in tins, is an exotic touch. It is dried fish impregnated with asafetida and definitely calls for an acquired taste.

Now that the frivolities have been dealt with, the curry comes next. This is an Indian recipe. It can be frozen, but since the flavor tends to fade, the seasonings should be corrected on reheating. The best way is to make it a day or two ahead of time and let it ripen in the refrigerator.

Madras Curry Good-quality lamb from the better portions of the beast, such as leg or shoulder, produces the best curry.

For each pound of meat, cut in bite-sized pieces, use:
   1 cup onion, chopped
   1 clove garlic, chopped or pressed
   1 small hot pepper pod, chopped
   3 tablespoons cooking oil (peanut, corn, etc.)
   1 tablespoon curry powder

1 cup water
2 tablespoons tomato paste
salt and lemon juice to taste

Fry the onion, garlic and pepper pod in the oil for 3 or 4 minutes. Stir in the curry powder and cook 3 or 4 minutes longer. The curry powder should be of the best possible quality, and that means real imported Indian curry. Add the meat and lightly brown it, pushing aside the onion so that it does not burn. Next add the water and tomato paste. Cover the pan and simmer very slowly for about an hour, or until the meat is thoroughly cooked. Now add the salt and lemon juice to taste.

The gravy should be moderately thick, but flour for thickening is taboo. If the gravy hasn't become concentrated enough by itself, add a little coconut cream (page 126) or cornstarch mixed with water. A pound of meat will produce 3 to 4 servings, so multiply everything according to your needs.

Cook the rice until the grains are dry and separated, and mound it in peaked hats on its serving platter; or make a ring of it surrounding the curry.

Puppadums are large, dried, flat, cracker-like biscuits. They are used to scoop up all the small bits and pieces of food. They may be bought in tins which include instructions for cooking them. Euphrates crackers or Fritos serve the same purpose and are easier to obtain.

Use frozen or canned fried onions rings, heated, of course, and crisped.

Eggplant may be oven-fried successfully. Pour cooking oil into a rimmed cookie sheet, to ⅛ inch

depth, and place it in the oven. Set the temperature at 400 degrees and get the fat very hot. While the fat is heating, dip peeled ¼-inch eggplant slices in beaten egg and then in cracker crumbs. Place in the hot fat and turn them once immediately and once again during cooking. (It is hard to state the timing definitely. Usually 5 minutes on a side will brown them nicely, but sometimes, for undetermined reasons, it takes longer.) When they are done, transfer the slices to absorbent paper, and return them to the oven with the heat off or very low to keep them warm until served.

Pineapple Quarters are attractive for dessert and can do double duty as a decoration when piled on a bed of cracked ice with fresh flowers tucked in here and there. Allow one quarter for each serving.

Cut fresh pineapple vertically in quarters. Cut through the green top, leaving attached, and trim any brown ends. Remove the core and free the pulp by cutting all around it close to the skin. Then cut the pulp, still in place in the shell, in thin crosswise slices. Pour a little rum or Cointreau over it; wrap the quarters in wax paper and chill thoroughly. Serve these with a fork and a caster of powdered sugar.

And so, GOD REST YE MERRY....Close at hand is the season of retrenchment, with hamburger and peanut butter resuming their esteemed positions, and the shedding greenery and fading boughs of holly going up in the smoke of another Christmas past. I hope your twelve days of Christmas have been cheered by these suggestions.

Index

Index

131

Index

Index

Index

Index

Index